TEASE

50 INSPIRED T-SHIRT TRANSFORMATIONS
BY SUPERSTARS OF ART, CRAFT & DESIGN

★ EDITED BY SARAH SOCKIT ★

PHOTOS BY DANIELLE ST. LAURENT

A Perigee Book

THE BERKLEY PUBLISHING GROUP
Published by the Penguin Group

Penguin Group (USA) Inc.
375 Hudson Street, New York, New York 10014, USA
Penguin Group (Canada), 90 Eglinton Avenue East, Suite 700, Toronto, Ontario M4P 2Y3, Canada
(a division of Pearson Penguin Canada Inc.)
Penguin Books Ltd., 80 Strand, London WC2R 0RL, England
Penguin Group Ireland, 25 St. Stephen's Green, Dublin 2, Ireland
(a division of Penguin Books Ltd.)
Penguin Group (Australia), 250 Camberwell Road, Camberwell, Victoria 3124, Australia
(a division of Pearson Australia Group Pty. Ltd.)
Penguin Books India Pvt. Ltd., 11 Community Centre, Panchsheel Park, New Delhi—110 017, India
Penguin Group (NZ), cnr. Airborne and Rosedale Roads, Albany, Auckland 1310, New Zealand
(a division of Pearson New Zealand Ltd.)
Penguin Books (South Africa) (Pty.) Ltd., 24 Sturdee Avenue, Rosebank, Johannesburg 2196, South Africa
Penguin Books Ltd., Registered Offices: 80 Strand, London WC2R 0RL, England

ART DIRECTION, COVER DESIGN, AND LAYOUT BY: **ARIN LoPRETE**
DESIGN, PRODUCTION, AND PHOTO RETOUCHING BY: **STEPHEN CONTI**
PHOTOS BY: **DANIELLE ST. LAURENT**

A Sockit Projects Book

Printing History
Perigee trade paperback edition / April 2006

 PERIGEE is a registered trademark of Penguin Group (USA) Inc.
The "P" design is a trademark belonging to Penguin Group (USA) Inc.

This book has been cataloged by the Library of Congress

printed in china
10 9 8 7 6 5 4 3 2 1

★★★★ TEASE ★★★★

TEASE
How to Use This Book

Icon Descriptions

Done in Under an Hour – Quick!

Done in an Afternoon – A longer commitment, but no big deal.

Basic Tool Kit – Includes sewing machine or needle and thread, fabric scissors, ruler, straight pins, tailor's chalk, iron, and ironing board.

Weekend Project – Make a commitment, but it'll be worth it.

Use What You Have – With a T-shirt and your basic tool kit, you're good to go!

Knitting Knowledge Helpful – Look it up online or ask your grandma; you'll need some knitting basics.

Special Shopping Trip Required – Unless you're a super crafter with a house full of materials, you'll need to shop for some extra supplies.

Crocheting Knowledge Helpful – Most basic crocheting techniques needed.

No Sewing Required – A little snip here, a couple of knots there and you're off!

Embroidery Knowledge Helpful – You can wing it, but embroidery knowledge could come in handy.

Sewing Level: Beginner – Hand or machine stitch straight lines; no complicated cuts or restructuring involved.

Cross Stitch Knowledge Helpful – It's not essential, but a few basics of cross stitch will make it easier.

Sewing Level: Experienced – More involved hand or machine stitches, trickier cuts or reconstruction.

Makes a Great Gift – It's not size-specific, and you made it with your own hands!

Difficulty Levels:

DIFFICULTY LEVEL	DIFFICULTY LEVEL	DIFFICULTY LEVEL	DIFFICULTY LEVEL
S	**M**	**L**	**XL**
NO SWEAT	GOOD TIME	GET BUSY	FOCUS

TEASE
Table of Contents

PREFACE

I'VE NEVER BEEN TO MAINE. But I have a well-worn, favorite royal-blue T-shirt with a white silkscreened outline of the state and "**MAINE**" spelled across it in a chunky font. T-shirts are like that—a comfortable collision of wearer and random design, message, or logo. Who doesn't have an old favorite in the back of their drawer that is no longer wearable "as is," but is impossible to part with for sentimental reasons? Add to that the plethora of promotional tees for bands, marathons, and corporate events, and we're neck-deep in logos and jersey fabric in dire need of recycling. This book is about reconfiguring those old favorites and reappropriating the corporate cast-offs by making them into something fresh, new, and hand-crafted.

TEASE features T-shirt transformations by 44 contributors —a cast of extraordinarily talented and creative artists, designers, and crafters. I assembled this crew by contacting people whose work I'd admired for years and inviting them to participate. The project quickly gained momentum and the sense of community grew as more people signed on and submitted their ideas. It became a life-sized game of connect the dots: people who had known of each other's work only through websites, blogs, and magazines were suddenly in a book together.

The enthusiasm and creativity was contagious. Shula Melamed showed up at our photo shoot with a 1950s hat box full of sliced and diced tees, wearing a "wife-beater" mysteriously knotted into a perfect-fit halter; Angela Adams, the designer of profound landscape-lush rugs, sent the cutest hand-stitched kitty; Georgie Greville, who was hired to model, brought her "Giddy Giddy Tee" to the shoot because she thought it would be perfect for the book; Jenny Mitchell, who had only a few days to come up with and write her project, invented a brilliant pizza analogy to make the instructions clear; DeEtte DeVille, busy working full-time as a family physician, made seven variations on her placemats so we'd "have options"; Debbie Stoller, editor of *BUST* magazine and author of the *Stitch 'N Bitch* series of books, used a long train ride to invent a whole new take on the tee—even though she doesn't consider herself a "T-shirt person."

As the projects rolled in, each package held a promise of something I imagined would be great, but which turned out to be cooler, smarter, and more accomplished than anything I expected. It seems that everyone felt the enlivening sense of creativity in transforming the banal or discarded into something fresh and new.

I hope that this book inspires you in the same way. You can follow the instructions laid out by our contributors or take them as a starting point for creating something original and all yours. **With a creative mind and a change in perspective, anything's possible!**

—SARAH SOCKIT

I WROTE AN INTRODUCTION TO THIS BOOK AND ALL I GOT WAS THIS LOUSY T-SHIRT

★ **BY SHOSHANA BERGER** ★

Scanner, Word-processing software, Clean, white or light-colored T-shirt, Iron-on transfer paper, Iron and ironing board.

1. Scan the intro pages into your computer. (If you don't have a scanner, use a copy shop's or a friend's services.)

2. In the word processing program of choice, view a page preview of the text section labeled **FRONT TOP**.

3. Now flip or mirror your block of text so that it will transfer in a readable way. It should be backward on screen.

4. Once the text looks OK, print it onto 1 sheet of iron-on transfer paper. Do the same with the text section labeled **FRONT BOTTOM**.

5. Now, following the same steps, print the section labeled **BACK TOP** and **BACK BOTTOM**. onto 2 more sheets, for a total of 4 iron-on blocks of text. Adjust your iron to its sizzling-est setting (no steam, please), and then press those inky sheets in order, as labeled, onto your freshly laundered tee.

Bonus for the unattached: *The text will be small and crowded, forcing people at parties to lean in close to read it.*

Before you go ripping it up and piecing it back together again, here are some things you should know about your T-shirt. It started as a not-very-clean thing. It started, if you must know, as dirty underwear. I don't mean the usual "dirty," as in you've worn it a couple of times and the underarms are looking a little canary. I mean dirty like Navy boys back in the 1880s, who didn't bathe for weeks. To cover their chest hair and take comfort in an extra layer of dry cloth, these salty dogs wore a woven-wool athletic tee under their uniforms, but it wouldn't be long before the U.S. Navy nixed the itchy wool and made the cotton crewneck standard-issue for all seamen. The whole "woven underwear" trend died out with the rise of industry and the advent of the cotton circular-knitting loom, which made possible the mass-production of clothing to which we've become accustomed and the finest in assembly-line hosiery factories on the Eastern Seaboard, churning out crisp cotton jerseys.

According to *The T-Shirt Book*, by Charlotte Brunel, the underwear company BVD started running its advertisements in newspapers as early as 1916; Sears, Roebuck, & Co. started pushing cotton sport shirts in their 1920s-era catalogs; and the timeless Hanes Corporation (now Fruit of the Loom) celebrated the poster boys of war in the '30s with their "gob" shirt, named after sailors. As the World War II–era machinery cranked into high gear, T-shirts were advertised as a way for the common man to identify with the courage and manhood of Army grunts. Brunel writes that Sears & Roebuck hawked their short-sleeved wares with the slogan, "You needn't be a soldier to have your own personal T-shirt." Soldiers in helmets and tees started making the fronts of magazine covers, and the cotton undershirt became the uniform of the ordinary man, fighting to defeat tyranny.

As the postwar Baby Boom generation came of age, the T-shirt lost much of its identification with recruits, becoming instead the symbol for disaffected youth and tough guys, as first Marlon Brando in *The Wild One* (1953), and then James Dean in *Rebel Without a Cause* (1955), became the T-shirt-and-leather-clad heartthrobs of Hollywood. Seeing teenaged girls swoon at matinees (and being no fools), young men everywhere followed suit. It wasn't just a guy thing, either. Gamines, like Jean Seberg in her *New York Herald Tribune* T-shirt in *Breathless*, made beatnik boyishness all the rage; voluptuous sirens, like Marilyn Monroe, created the opposite effect by wearing curve-hugging tees tucked into belted jeans. Either way, the shirt became synonymous with a generation bent on unbuttoning the stiff cultural mores of the past. Of course, the people in charge—parents, principals, politicians—didn't like it one bit. There was something anti-authority in the short sleeves that celebrated the working man, and during the McCarthy years, the tee smacked a little too much of social equality.

But socialist paranoia didn't keep publicity departments from using the T-shirt to promote their companies' brands. The 1950s saw the first universities and sports teams printing their crests, numbers, and logos onto T-shirts, so that alums and fans could wear their affiliations on their sleeves—and chests, and backs. Then the '60s hit, and with so many causes and so few hours in the day to sit in and be civilly disobedient, the T-shirt became a kind of wearable sandwich board. Hippies and barnstormers alike used the standard textile printing process of silkscreening, as well as newer, faster methods of hot-image transfer, like embossing with flock printing or bubble coating to create the bold, black "peace" signs, and the defiant, grizzled face of Che Guevara looking up from under a beret. Those, along with the revival of old folk craft in psychedelic, rainbow-colored tie-dyes, are visual flashpoints of an era we can never forget.

Fully acceptable as casual outerwear in schools by the early '70s, the cotton tee became ubiquitous in the American closet, and women's magazines declared the T-shirt a staple that would never go out of fashion. This was the decade in which the tee became a major advertising vehicle, with nearly every consumer brand from Coke to Levi's to Harley-Davidson slapping shirts with their logos. Iron-on letters and decals (Hello, disco glitter! Unicorns! Rolling Stones Warhol lips!) were sold in shops that featured hundreds of T-shirts and baseball ringers lining the walls.

Although do-it-yourself modifications started in the '60s with tie-dyes, it wasn't until London punks started thrashing their tees that the age of customization truly began. The Sex Pistols were probably the most famous example of the first massive reconstruction of the shirt. No surprise then that their manager, Malcolm McLaren, had been trained as a clothing designer and owned a shop in London with Vivienne Westwood. The image of Sid Vicious scowling for the camera, wearing T-shirts that had been ripped at the neck, breast, and belly button, became punk's sartorial battle cry: Live hard. Self-destruct. As with the preceding generation of Baby Boomers—who'd seen James Dean die in a motorcycle accident at 24 years old, after his own incitement to "live fast, die young, and leave a good-looking corpse"— this new breed of youth used the ripped, safety-pinned, and shredded tee with the anarchist logo, "God Save the Queen," and radical regalia as the badge of an anti-establishment attitude.

[END FRONT BOTTOM]

[BEGIN BACK TOP]

The post-"Me" decade had a love affair with the T-shirt that went well beyond imitating the pop stars piped into suburban living rooms on MTV. As the academe swooned under the influence of poststructuralist and deconstructionist theories of language from France, couture lines, like Comme des Garçons, sent asymmetrical tees down the runway. Some designers revamped and reduced the shirt into such an abstract shape that it resembled sculpture more than clothing.

Music and fashion aside, however, movies continued to set broader trends. Take *Flashdance*: Jennifer Beals's signature ripped sweatshirt-and-tee combo instantly fossilized the collared shirt as teenagers everywhere started ripping off sleeves and necklines to emulate the welder-turned-dancer. *Fame*, which touted a life of expression through freedom of movement and body awareness, stoked the *Flashdance* coals, making sporty-cotton everything hot. Then, in the late '80s, hip-hop hit the scene, and with it an obsession with blingy logo clothing. Suddenly, T-shirt chests flaunted athletic brands, like Adidas and Puma, with the fashion world quick on the uptake, splashing the intertwined Ds and Gs of Gucci and Dolce on everything.

Virtually every epochal shift is reflected on T-shirts; the digital age of personal computers, email, and the World Wide Web is no exception. *Wired* magazine founder Louis Rossetto may have famously declared that the new technology would have an impact equivalent to the discovery of fire, but to the average T-shirt-wearer, new technology meant more avenues for image manipulation. Gen Xers, who'd graduated with "useless" liberal arts degrees, suddenly found jobs at start-ups as graphic designers and content providers—and these startups were not officially started up until they had a T-shirt emblazoned with a spunky tagline. With this digitally enabled breed of image-makers came a wave of customized T-shirts that brandished everything from subversive spins on corporate logos ("Enjoy Cocaine" in the shape of a Coca-Cola logo is the classic) to custom designs tweaked in Photoshop.

[END BACK TOP]

[BEGIN BACK BOTTOM]

With concerts, companies, and colleges each producing their own must-have swag, most of us have collected enough T-shirts to clothe a developing country. In a funny twist, the age of swag is giving way to a reactionary consciousness that is no longer thrilled with the chilly perfection of digital imagery and mass-production. With so many people stuck in point-and-click careers by the turn of the millennium, a hankering to create—or at least own—things made by hand started influencing the way T-shirts looked. This mindset, along with a sharpened focus on total recycling and making better use of our resources, has created an entirely new trend in T-shirt fashion: the artist's limited edition of hand-stitched, dyed, or printed T-shirts. What better raw material than the mountains of T-shirts languishing in our closets?

Many of the contributors in this book are frontrunners of the reuse-oriented neo-craft movement, which lives in grassroots communities such as Debbie Stoller's knitting circle, Stitch 'N Bitch (knithappens.com), magazines like *Bust* and *ReadyMade*, and, of course, blogs. Stoller has made it her mission to re-appropriate the domestic arts for a generation of women who like to make stuff, but who chafe at craft's pre-feminist associations with being the purview of bored, homebound, and non-careerist women. Callie Janoff, founder of the Church of Craft (churchofcraft.org), has founded a new religion around the creative process, a congregation that meets in cities across the country to make stuff together. Leah Kramer's Craftster (craftster .org) is a near-Talmudic resource for do-it-yourselfers who post project pictures, tutorials, and tips in an open-source forum. Todd Oldham, though already sainted by the fashion world, still finds that our most down-at-heel cultural artifacts (like groupie tees) can be boiled down into a rich broth of signifiers and associations.

The new arts-and-crafts movement has yielded an incredible bounty, which eagle-eyed retailers are eager to harvest for mass consumption. One can now find ersatz versions of the raw-edged, handcrafted T-shirt at major malls across America. How do basement designers respond to the copycats? By getting even more obscure and inventive and limiting themselves to micro-production runs that are sold only from Web storefronts or blogs. Even better, some crafters have taken to giving buyers the option of personalizing their own shirts or subscribing to an annual, limited-edition series of hand-printed shirts.

The customization trend, which forward-thinking consumer-electronics makers have been quick to pick up (engraved iPods, cell-phone ring tones), gives consumers a way to stamp their identities on their gear. The T-shirt world has taken customization even further, so that the most coveted item is one that no one else has. The result is a new breed of T-shirt that retains the carbon-based warmth of a human maker, something slightly off-center and frayed—un-reproducibly imperfect.
[END BACK BOTTOM]

Enter the 44 contributors who make up this book, each one an artist, designer, or do-it-yourself tinkerer who's turned his or her attention to the tee. In a move that befits our times and our subject—the democratic emblem of the everyday—they've all agreed to share a few trade secrets with us. Some have found wearables within the wearable, making T-shirt scarves, blouses, or skirts. Others have spared us more closet stuffers and instead shared tips for turning our avalanche of cotton into items with a household purpose, such as placemats, pillows, and rugs. Where do you come in? Use these ideas to transform that drawer of outdated band and brand tees you've been keeping around for God knows how long (or why). Each project includes easy-to-follow, step-by-step instructions and diagrams for making stuff you won't believe you've lived without (what is life without a T-shirt tote bag?).

TEASE is exactly that—a playful prod that gets you off the couch and into the craft corner. Once you've trial-and-errored your way through a few mods, we hope you'll think of these projects as jumping-off points—a few bright ideas to inspire your own reinventions. Like your tie-dyeing, neck-ripping, safety-pinning forbears, think of that outdated, over-branded T-shirt as your canvas. You are the Cub Scout of the closet. Go in bravely, and make stuff.

FLOWER CUTOUT TEE

This project makes use of the template of your choice. If you don't know where to find a fun template, check your local fabric store, especially the quilting section, where there are usually a bunch of super-durable plastic templates that work great for this adventure.

Once you master the art of the Flower Cutout Tee, try the same technique on other items. It's a simple way to add interest to almost anything: skirts, hoodies, shorts, tanks, totes, scarves, and even pillows. Templates make things so easy!

Alison Rose (alisonrose.com), the creative collaboration of **Alison Bartlett** and **Nicholas Nocera,** features unique, embellished T-shirts, handbags, paper goods, and accessories. Each piece is handmade and individually designed, which means nothing is mass-produced or manufactured.

Alison and Nicholas met while studying art and fashion at Kent State University. They started alisonrose.com in the fall of 2003 as a way to share the products Alison had been creating for herself, her family, and her friends. Alison has always loved making things and Nicholas has always been interested in art and design. Alison and Nicholas live in Columbus, Ohio, in a cozy downtown apartment, where they're always thinking up new ideas for their shop.

DIRECTIONS

What You'll Need: Prewashed T-shirt, Flower template for cutout design (quilting templates work great), One 12-by-12-inch piece of lightweight iron-on adhesive paper (available at any fabric store), One 12-by-12-inch piece of lightweight interfacing, One 12-by-12-inch piece of prewashed fun fabric, Thread in contrasting color

1. Turn your T-shirt inside out, smooth it onto a flat work surface, and arrange your flower template on the tee where you'd like your cutout design to appear. Using tailor's chalk, trace the flower outline onto your tee. You can also freehand your own design if you have a flair for that kind of thing.

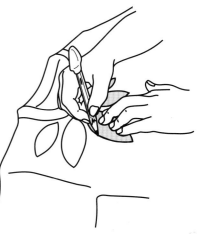

2. Place the adhesive paper—smooth side up, adhesive side down—over the pattern you just traced onto your tee. Use a pencil to trace a blob shape about an inch larger than the entire flower pattern onto the paper back of the adhesive, and then cut it out. No, really, cut it out, or I'm telling Mom!

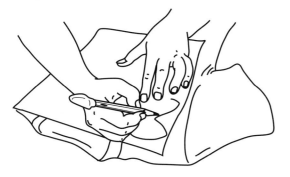

3. Lay the tee on the ironing board, and then place the cutout adhesive—smooth side up, adhesive side down—over your traced shapes. Make sure the adhesive shape is lined up over your design, and then carefully press with a hot iron. Let cool. Before you pull off the adhesive backing, use a ruler and pencil to mark the grain of the T-shirt onto the adhesive back, and then make a note for top and bottom. This will help when you put your fabric in place later, especially if you're working with a striped fabric and want to make sure the stripes are going the right way.

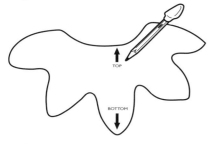

4. After the adhesive is cool and you've made your marks, carefully peel up the backing of the adhesive paper, making sure it comes off in one piece, and set it aside; you'll need it later.

5. With sharp fabric scissors, very carefully and cleanly cut the T-shirt and the attached adhesive material along your traced pattern lines. You'll be left with a bunch of template-shaped holes that are sticky on the inside of the shirt.

6. Next you'll add the contrasting fabric that makes this shirt design so cool. Start by stabilizing your fun fabric. Smooth it out onto your work surface, wrong-side down, and then lay the interfacing on the fabric, pressing with a hot iron to fuse the interfacing to the fabric. You now have a stiff piece of fabric that will be much easer to attach to your T-shirt.

7. Find that paper adhesive backing you set aside a few steps ago, and lay it onto the interfacing side of the fabric. Be sure to follow the top, bottom, and grain markings you made earlier. Using the paper as a template, use a pencil to trace the template onto your fabric, adding a 1/8-inch margin all the way around. Using fabric scissors, cut out the shape you just drew on the fabric. You can now throw away the adhesive backing.

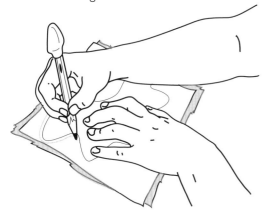

8. You're almost finished! Lay your T-shirt, still inside out, onto your ironing board, so that the layer with the cutouts is smoothed flat on the board, in a single layer. Place the fabric shape over the cutout, fabric side down, interfacing side up, so that the right side of the stiff, fun fabric is touching the sticky side of the cutouts on the T-shirt. Carefully press with iron, and then allow to cool. Turn your tee right side out and press it again from the outside. You have just fused your stiff, fun fabric to your sticky, cutout tee.

9. Now it's time for the grand finale—a little sewing. Using contrasting thread, stitch around each opening, about 1/4 inch from the edge, making sure your stitches go through both layers of fabric, the T-shirt and the fabric underneath. Try to make your stitches nice and even—not only are you backing up the adhesive fusion with a little stitchery, but you are also adding a fancy decorative element. Once you've sewn around each cutout, you're ready to go.

Wash your tee as you normally would—the hand stitching will hold the fabric in place, even after multiple washings, when the adhesive has worn away.

CUTOUT CAT

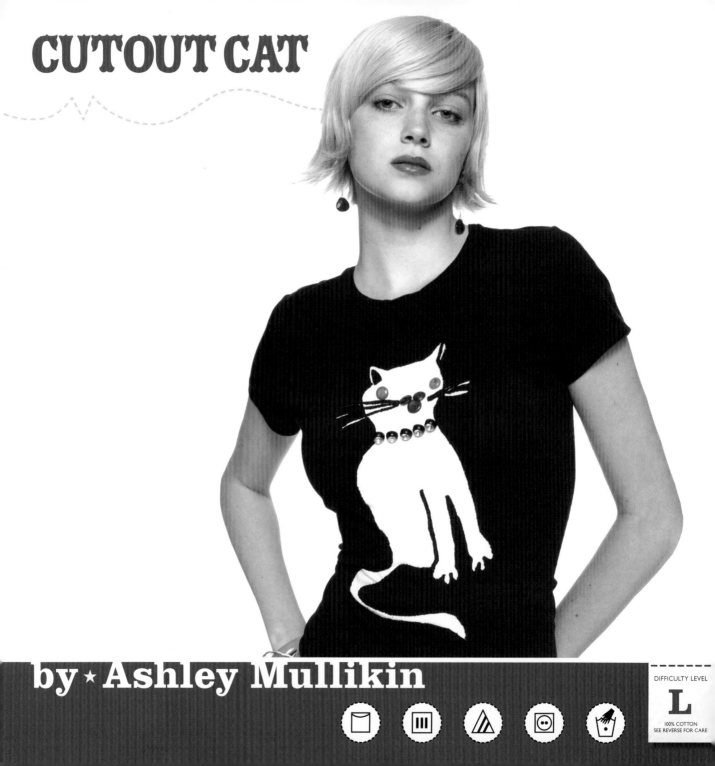

by ★ Ashley Mullikin

DIFFICULTY LEVEL

L

100% COTTON
SEE REVERSE FOR CARE

No one should have to wear a plain T-shirt when making your own personalized design is so easy, especially with this appliqué method, which is designed for success.

After drawing my favorite pet on my favorite tee, it only took an extra layer of fabric, a few zigzags on the ol' Singer, and some embellishments from grandma's button jar to make my cat, Annie, appear before my eyes. Of course, your appliqué design can be your name, a friend's name, or a volleyball—whatever it takes to make this project your very own.

Ashley Mullikin graduated from Pratt Institute in Brooklyn, New York, with a degree in fashion design; she is now a clothing designer in Minneapolis. Originally from Livermore, California, Ashley enjoys playing the bass guitar, swimming, and skateboarding.

DIRECTIONS

What You'll Need: 2 T-shirts, Paper (optional), Colored thread, Buttons (optional)

1. On a sturdy, flat surface, such as a desk or table, layer 2 T-shirts, one inside the other, smoothing both layers flat.

2. Using tailor's chalk, draw your design on the top-layer T-shirt. You may want to make a paper pattern first, and then trace around it on the tee; just remove the pattern after you trace it, before you begin to sew.

3. Using straight pins, pin the two layers of fabric flat around the design. You can pin the layers together on the inside or outside of the design, but be sure not to catch the back side of the T-shirt with the pins.

4. With a sewing machine, zigzag stitch through the two layers of fabric, using the lines you drew as a guide; the zigzag stitch allows the T-shirt to remain flexible and stretchy after you are finished working. Make sure that the outline of the motif is sewn all the way around and that both layers of T-shirt are completely connected. If you're feeling whimsical, use thread in fun colors to stitch your design.

5. To expose the under-layer of fabric and make your stitched design resemble an appliqué, use extra-sharp fabric scissors to cut away the top layer of fabric within your stitched lines, being careful not to snip the zigzag stitching or penetrate the lower layer of cloth. Try to be neat and tidy with your scissoring so that your appliqué's edge is clean-cut and professional looking.

6. Turn both shirts inside out and cut away the excess under-layer fabric on the inside of the T-shirt. Be careful to cut only outside your stitched lines. When you are finished, you'll have one mostly whole T-shirt, with a design-shaped hole in the middle, backed by the different-colored T-shirt fabric showing from the inside.

7. Turn the shirt right-side out and add buttons for extra decoration.

Behold the power of creativity!

E-Z SILKSCREEN

by ★ Bari Schlosser Franklin

DIFFICULTY LEVEL

Silkscreen printing is a mysterious process that transfers paint to a surface (in this case, a T-shirt) through a stencil printed on a fine, fabric mesh that has been stretched tightly over a frame. The printer uses a squeegee to squish paint through the open areas on the stenciled mesh. Solid areas in the stencil block the ink from getting through the screen, while open areas allow the ink to flow through to the printing surface, producing a print.

I love to screen-print, but I don't have a studio set up where I can burn my designs onto silkscreens, and I never get around to schlepping across town to the screen-print supply shop to have them made. Instead, I use a blank screen in combination with easy-to-make stencils. All you'll need is one silkscreen, and you can create endless designs without chemicals or hassle. Talk about instant gratification!

Bari Schlosser Franklin, who lives in a small house in Greenpoint, Brooklyn, with her husband, Stash, and their offspring, Ariel and Ezra, designs T-shirts, graphics, and fabrics for companies in the U.S. and Japan. She also works to develop products that help sustain natural resources; she directed Renewable Brooklyn, an outdoor summer festival that promoted environmental concerns in the borough.

DIRECTIONS

What You'll Need: T-shirt, Paper (for cutting out your stencil) or other flat objects to use as stencils, Water-soluble silkscreen print ink for fabric (available at art supply stores or silkscreen supply stores), Something in which to mix the paint, such as a disposable plastic bowl, Wooden silkscreen frame with mesh screen (available at art supply stores), Silkscreen squeegee, Newspaper (for practicing)

1. Decide what you'd like to print on your T-shirt. You'll need something you can use as a stencil: either a pre-cut shape (such as a Valentine doily), a shape you've cut out yourself, or a flat object (like a leaf).

2. In a disposable or paint-safe container, mix the silkscreen ink colors to achieve the hue(s) you'd like to use. If you're a novice at color mixing, pick up an inexpensive color wheel at the art-supply store.

3. Lay your T-shirt on a flat surface and smooth out any wrinkles. Select the area where you'd like your design to go, and place the stencil on that area. You can layer several stencils at once or just use one stencil at a time.

4. Lay the blank screen on top of the stencil, being careful not to disturb it.

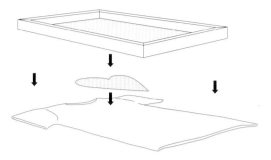

5. Now for the ink: Spreading ink evenly across the screen can be tricky, even with a silkscreen squeegee, and it may take a little practice to get just the right amount of ink through your screen and onto your printing surface. Try practicing several times on newspaper before attempting to screen your design onto a beloved (or expensive) T-shirt. Once you've perfected your squeegee pull, you can print on your shirt.

6. When you're ready, pour the ink in a line across the top of the screen and pull the paint down the screen with the squeegee.

7. Once the ink on your shirt is completely dry, heat-set the paint by ironing the back side of the shirt. (Never iron directly on the paint.)

The screen and stencils can be used multiple times. Since you're using water-soluble ink (which dries quickly), be sure to wash your screen immediately after you finish using it. Otherwise, the ink will dry in the mesh, rendering your screen useless. I wash my screen in the bathtub, but a large sink will do.

HULA
LAMPSHADE

DIFFICULTY LEVEL

S

100% COTTON
SEE REVERSE FOR CARE

Why should people (and dogs) be the only ones who get to wear T-shirts? This low-tech solution for a quick-fix lampshade brings the joy of soft cotton to every room in your house. If you change décor like you change your socks, you can even make several—redesign on a whim.

We think this project would look amazing with several different tees sewn together like patchwork. Or you can do this quickie version—we did ours in less than two hours. Just think, yours is going to look ten tons cuter!

Chris Bick and **Keith Carollo** met in Chicago; on their first date, they went to a carnival, where they rode the Ferris wheel until Keith threw up. Despite that dubious beginning, they found they shared a passion for design and a belief that it should be as fun as an old musical or a modern music video. By 1998, they were selling disposable drink coasters off the back of a bike in SoHo, and the **fredflare** (fredflare .com) line was born.

Named after the sparkling style of Fred Astaire, fredflare is an ever-changing collection of Chris and Keith's favorite things. The online boutique has grown to include stationery, home décor, and accessories.

Chris loves Madonna and sharks; Keith loves Nancy Drew and hula hoops. They both adore *Breakfast at Tiffany's* and cheeseburgers (in that order).

DIRECTIONS

What You'll Need: Plain T-shirt, Lampshade and a fun lamp base, Large needle, Yarn, T-shirt with a groovy logo or design or a piece of interesting fabric, Masking tape

1. First stop—dressing room! Put the tee on your shade and see how it fits. To keep things simple, choose a shirt that's close to the size of the shade. We found a tee that fit perfectly, so the shade would have one continuous piece of fabric at the bottom. This means no seam and very little sewing.

2. Arrange the shirt so that the bottom hem seam lines up with the bottom of the shade. Cut off any extra T-shirt fabric above the shade, leaving 1 1/2 inches in excess. Also, cut off the upper portion of the shirt and the sleeves.

7. Fold the raw edge at the top of the T-shirt over the edge of the lampshade and secure it on the inside of the shade with masking tape. (Our tape job? Not so neat. Do as we say, not as we do.)

8. Add a flourish! We *love* flourishes—they're a great way to camouflage little mistakes. Who would look past the plastic lei to inspect our sewing technique? I mean, really!

That's it! Stick a fork in it—it's *done*!

3. Remove tee from shade and trim any rough edges. Delicious!

4. Using a large needle and yarn, whipstitch the bottom part of the tee.

5. Place the T-shirt on the shade again and decide which part will be in front. Remove it, and sew or embellish the tee any way you desire. Sew on a cool logo you cut from a 2nd shirt or use an interesting shape cut from fabulous fabric. We used a sewing machine to stitch on the Waikiki part (see picture), but you could probably do just as well by hand. Here's a tip: since you know you're probably not going to use the arms of the tee, they make great scraps you can use to practice your technique. Time to sew (a valuable skill for every girl and boy)!

6. Now put the tee back on the lampshade and arrange it to look adorable. You're almost finished!

SOUVENIR TEE BAG

by ★ Donna Jairdullo

DIFFICULTY LEVEL

As a big fan of indie rock, I spent a lot of time in the early '90s going to concerts, bringing home T-shirts from my favorite groups. Back then, concert tees were always large or extra-large. One size fits all? Hardly! I bought them anyway, despite their bad fit, because they're such great mementos from shows I loved.

Eventually, since I was just drowning in their hugeness, I ended up getting rid of a lot of good shirts. Later on, I realized that I could recycle these shirts into another form, which was the inspiration for creating T-shirt bags. Now, if I could only get back all those T-shirts I gave away…

Donna Jairdullo, a New Jersey native and wannabe New Yorker, spent most of college mastering the arts of part-time record-store clerking and indie-rock geek chic; she graduated from a New Jersey university with a BA in Fine Art. She later worked in New York City magazine publishing before taking a geographic leap to Los Angeles. After a brief stint in the Golden State, she returned to the NY metro area to take up a gig in marketing.

Donna's first and only true love is music, and she spends an inordinate amount of time listening to and seeking out new tunes. Music has been a huge inspiration in her quest for all things crafty. Souvenir, her hand-made tote venture, is the culmination of her passion for road trips, music, and all things vintage.

DIRECTIONS

What You'll Need: Oversized T-shirt, Tape measure, 3/4-inch fusible bias tape (silver) or ribbon, 7-inch plastic or wood purse handles (round or D-ring)

⋆   ⋆   ⋆

1. Starting at the side seam of the shirt, cut the front of the shirt away from the back, sleeves, and collar, so that the back and front of the T-shirt become separate pieces.

2. Your tote will vary in size, depending upon how large your shirt is. However, you'll need at least 5 inches of plain fabric at the top of your shirt for attaching handles to the bag. If the design on your tee is located too close to the top of the shirt, remove 5 inches from the bottom of your shirt panels, pin these fabric strips, right sides together, to the main body of the front and back of your shirt, respectively, and sew them into place, leaving a 1/2-inch seam allowance. You now have more material at the top for attaching the handles.

3. Before you go any further, you'll want to decorate the front of your bag (you can't do much to it after you've sewn the pieces together). In my example, I'm using the silver bias tape to cover the seam on the front panel of the bag (I had to complete Step 2). Center the fusible bias tape over the seam and iron. To make the binding more decorative, topstitch the tape on the top and bottom edges. Slick, Rick!

4. Next, cut the front panel into a 22-by-17 1/2-inch piece; your bag will be slightly smaller once sewn. Cut the back panel to match the front panel in size.

5. Pin the front and back pieces together, right sides facing, along the bottom and side edges of your bag. Stop pinning the sides approximately 5 inches from the top of the bag, so that there's excess fabric for attaching the handles.

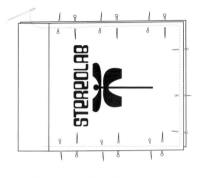

6.

Sew the bottom and sides of the bag, leaving a 1/2-inch seam allowance. Stop sewing 5 inches from the top of the bag. Your bag will be inside out, so now's the time to turn it right-side out. Looking good, yes?

7. With your bag right-side out, take one handle and place it on the inside of the back panel of your bag. Fold 2 inches of the material over the handle and pin at each end of the bag. Working from the ends, gather and pin the fabric toward the center of the handle, gathering material as you go along.

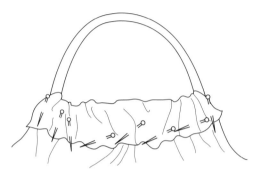

8. Once all the fabric is pinned, attach the handle by sewing a straight stitch as close to the edge of the handle as possible. Then, flip your bag over and repeat these steps for attaching the second handle. Way to get a handle on it!

9. The material on the inside of the bag under the handles will be ruffled. To give your bag a little more polish, sew the edge of that raw, loose material with a zigzag stitch.

Your bag is now complete and looking snazzy. Tell your friends to go make their own!

PING-PONG BALL NECKLACE

by Jennifer Perkins

I've seen lots of fabulous fabric-covered, beaded necklaces in fashion magazines, and since everything is bigger in Texas (including the fashion), I wanted my beads to be big—really big. I racked my brain for an idea, until pow! Ping-pong balls popped into my head.

My mom, sister, and I all tweaked and contributed to this necklace. It's definitely different! This idea also works well as a belt, or with a few less balls, you can even wear it as a headband, Frida Kahlo–style. Your serve!

Disillusioned when a degree in psych landed her a job as a secretary, **Jennifer Perkins** decided to focus on her lifelong passion: making jewelry. She quit her job and launched Naughty Secretary Club (naughtysecretaryclub.com), which combines all her favorite things: music, pop culture, and vintage goodies. Naughty Secretary Club has been featured in *Glamour, ELLEgirl, Lucky,* and many more magazines. You can see Jennifer in action with other members of the Austin Craft Mafia on *Stylelicious* and as the host of *CraftLab*, both on the DIY Network.

Jennifer lives in Austin, Texas, with her hubby, doggie, and kitty. Sometimes she tinkers with the record label she and her husband own, called Has Anyone Ever Told You? (hasanyoneevertoldyou.com).

DIRECTIONS

What You'll Need: T-shirt (if you can, use a wild-animal pattern, like I did!), 9 ping-pong balls, Twist ties, Pink jewelry wire, Black thread, Pink satin ribbon

1. Start by cutting off the bottom 5 inches of the T-shirt, leaving you a 5-inch-wide band of fabric. Next, cut this band along the seam on one side to create a single long piece of fabric.

2. Line the ping-pong balls up along the wrong side of the fabric (if you have cats, you might want to put them outside so they don't interfere with this part). Fold and pull the fabric around the balls carefully, and twist-tie the fabric between the balls to section them off (see diagram). Don't worry—the ugly twist ties are there just to hold the fabric in place.

3. Wrap pink jewelry wire between each ball, removing the twist ties as you go. Much better!

4. Adjust the length of the necklace by trimming some of the excess T-shirt material at each end.

5. To make ties to fasten the ends of the necklace around your neck, first glue pink ribbon around two ping-pong balls, allowing the ribbon to dry until it is completely secure. Next, cut 2 circles, 5 inches in diameter, from the remaining T-shirt fabric. Put one of the ribbon-covered balls in the center of each circle, gather the fabric tightly around the ball and tie it in place using a twist tie. The long end of the ribbon will extend out beyond the tie. As you did in Step 3, replace the twist tie with the much more attractive jewelry wire. Your ping-pong ribbon-ties are ready to attach to your necklace.

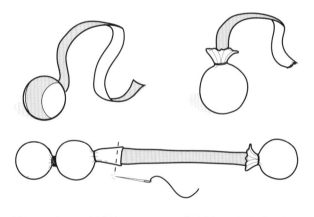

8. Attach the ribbon ties to each end of the T-shirt necklace with a straight stitch on the sewing machine (you could also use a needle and thread if you prefer).

9. Fasten the necklace by tying the ribbon and letting the two end balls hang down your back.

How's that for kooky fun?

iPOD COZY

by ★ Scott Cronick

DIFFICULTY LEVEL

M

100% COTTON
SEE REVERSE FOR CARE

I've been a T-shirt recycler for a couple of years now. It all started when I was working as a wardrobe stylist on one of those entertainment talk shows. The host I dressed loved wearing vintage tees, but he would only wear them once, so the wardrobe closet quickly began to overflow with T-shirts. What to do? Turn them into pillows, of course! I started making vintage T-shirt pillows for friends and people around the office. They were a huge success, so my evenings were soon consumed with cutting, stitching, and stuffing T-shirts.

Being the impatient person I am, I quickly got bored with the pillows, but still wanted to play with creating something else from the T-shirts, so I figured out the fusing process used in this project. Fusing the T-shirts to various other fabrics gives them new life and makes them stronger and more durable. Now, I make bags, pillows, iPod cozies, and duvet covers out of vintage tees from around the world and sell them out of my East Village store, Cronick Valentine.

For **Scott Cronick,** design has always been his personal mode of expression. His East Village boutique, Cronick Valentine (cronickvalentine.com), is a home for the utterly unique—not only a showcase for emerging musical and artistic talent, but home to Scott's watch designs and his popular Pig-Your-T program, a service that transforms customers' favorite T-shirts into one-of-a-kind iPod cases and handbags.

Before teaming up with Valentina Ryan to create Cronick Valentine, Scott worked as a wardrobe assistant at *Late Night With Conan O'Brien* and as a star-dresser at *Saturday Night Live,* and he was the New York stylist for *Access Hollywood.*

DIRECTIONS

What You'll Need: Permanent marker, 12-inch square of clear vinyl, Two 12-inch squares of fusible webbing with paper on one side and spun glue on the other (available at any craft store), 12-inch square of felt (any color), 12-inch square of flannel, T-shirt, 1 1/2-inch piece of 1-inch wide sew-in Velcro

1. Using the permanent marker and ruler, draw a 10-by-3 1/2-inch rectangle on the vinyl. To one of the rectangle's shorter sides, add a square with 1 1/2-inch sides. Label the other short side of the rectangle "top." Cut out the whole rectangle/square combo, in one piece, and set it aside.

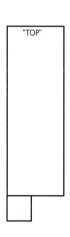

2. Place one of the fusible webbing squares on the felt, paper side up. Using an iron set to "no steam," heat-set the fusible webbing to the felt. Once the felt has cooled, remove the paper backing, and then place the flannel square on top of the fusible webbing you just fused to the felt, right side up, making a little flannel/fusible webbing/felt sandwich. Use the iron to heat-set the flannel to the felt. To ensure you get a good bond, be sure to hold the iron for at least 10 seconds over the entire piece. On the reverse side of the felt, heat-set the 2nd piece of fusible webbing paper side up. Do not remove the paper. Set aside your little fabric/ webbing sandwich.

3. Retrieve the clear vinyl pattern you made in Step 1 and place it on your T-shirt, covering the portion that you would like to appear on your iPod case (fun graphic, sardonic logo, wry witticism). As you place the pattern, keep in mind that the short side of the rectangle without the square will become the top of the case, and the portion of the T-shirt visible through the vinyl will appear on the finished product. Now cut around the pattern, leaving at least 1 inch of extra T-shirt all the way around. Remove the vinyl pattern and set it aside.

4. Remove the paper from the flannel/felt sandwich you made in Step 2—save the paper backing, as you will need it in just a moment. Set the bit of tee you just cut out on top of the felt side of the flannel/felt sandwich. Remember that piece of backing I told you to save? Set it on top of the T-shirt fabric, which will protect your tee from the scorching iron. Heat-set the T-shirt to the felt by pressing with a dry, hot iron. Voila! Your club sandwich has just become a double-decker pressed panini.

5. Pin your vinyl pattern-piece back on to the fused T-shirt, in the same position it was in earlier. Using scissors, trim away the excess fabric around the pattern. Unpin and toss the pattern—you're done with it!

6. On the top left corner of the T-shirt side of the iPod case, stitch the female (fuzzy) piece of the Velcro. On the flannel side of the 1 1/2-inch tab at the top of the iPod case stitch the male piece of Velcro. Ah, it's a match made in iPod heaven!

7. Using the satin stitch on your sewing machine (or a very close zigzag), stitch along the top edge of the iPod case. Be sure to actually go over the edge of the fabric, creating a finished edge. Using the same stitch, finish the bottom of the iPod case (including the 1 1/2-inch tab).

8. Fold the case in half, making a little pouch, and then satin-stitch all the way up the sides.

Clip the threads and crank it up, because you are done!

FOLD HERE

PLACEMATS

by DeEtta DeVille

DIFFICULTY LEVEL

We love and honor our T-shirts. Their graphics testify to our ideologies and accomplishments, and their comfort reminds us that fashion doesn't have to hurt.

Sadly, you only have one torso, so in the likely event you own more T-shirts than you could possibly wear this month, here's a simple sewing project that will turn your tees (and even your used jeans) into a distinctive set of placemats. When they get dirty, you can throw them in the washing machine, just as you would jeans and a T-shirt.

Get crazy-crafty with your designs. It's simplest to use the front of a T-shirt cut to the correct size, but combining different colors and graphics can yield some fabulously ironic results. I recommend using a single piece of T-shirt as the base, and then attaching other desired bits using appliqué or adhesives. Just be careful not to make your placemats so layered and lumpy that your glass of breakfast juice tips over!

DIRECTIONS

What You'll Need: 1 T-shirt for each placemat, 1 19-by-13-inch piece of denim or canvas (a leg of used jeans works well) for each placemat

DeEtte DeVille has lived in New Jersey, New York, Montana, Utah, Texas, and California. She claims Washoe, Montana, as her home base, but currently lives in New York City.

While training as a family-practice physician at Loma Linda University, DeEtte's interest (and bachelor's degree) in design kept her involved in retail textile projects, such as her infamous sock monkey jackets and vibrator cozies. She continues to explore fine art, fashion, and houseware projects using reclaimed fabric—and although the sewing machine her mom gave her as a medical-school graduation gift stays out and active in her tiny Manhattan apartment, she maintains her day job as a doctor.

1. Cut out the side seams of the T-shirt, removing the back from the front. Set aside the plain side of the shirt and eyeball the front piece, deciding how you'd like to position your tee's design on your placemat.

2. Cut out a 19-by-13-inch piece from the design side, making sure you're placing the graphic where you want on your finished placemat. If the shirt is small, cut out a 19-by-13-inch piece from a larger, less interesting tee, and then attach the design piece to the larger piece with spray adhesive or appliqué.

3. Match together the wrong sides of the denim and tee fabric. Pin the edges, keeping the pins within 1/2 inch of the fabric edge.

4. Sew together the edges of the mat, leaving a 1/2-inch seam allowance and a 2-inch opening along one side. Trim the corner seam allowance at a 45-degree angle.

5. Turn the placemat right-side out through the 2-inch opening, and then press the mat flat.

6. For a style that closes up the 2-inch opening and also helps the placemat lie flat, topstitch a border on the mat, 1/4 inch from the edge.

Now, stand back and admire your new conversation piece—no more boring dinners here!

PEEP - SHOW TEE

by ★ Katherine Shaughnessy

DIFFICULTY LEVEL

M

100% COTTON
SEE REVERSE FOR CARE

This is my minimalist, crafter version of a slasher T-shirt. When I started this shirt, I had just finished a small painting with similar holes "machine gunned" across a pink and glittered canvas. It was a fun piece, and I thought: Why not punch holes in clothes? Embroidering the holes ensures they stay put after washing and don't get any bigger.

If you're really into this project, how about covering an entire shirt—or skirt, or even pants—in these embroidered holes? Not into white? Then take a red T-shirt and embroider hot-pink holes. Or make a bunch of different-sized holes along the bottom edge of an old T-shirt. Or fill only the sleeves with holes (you'll need a very little hoop to do this).

A warning for the hairy-chested: Maybe this isn't the project for you. If you're into the design, but a bit too hairy (or prudish), wear a contrasting tank underneath; the under-color will really pop.

Go ahead—make a hole-y mess, already.

Katherine Shaughnessy learned to sew at age 5. She got her first pair of eyeglasses at age 6, and her sewing noticeably improved. Katherine soon founded her neighborhood Nature & Crafts Club and eventually attended graduate school at the Art Institute of Chicago.

Later, while living in a chalet in Michigan, Katherine created Doegirl (doegirl.com). She traveled the country in a van for a year, painting murals of trees and making miniature dioramas of make-believe landscapes. Eventually, she landed in the desert-mountains of far West Texas, where she become a chicken farmer who also designs crewel embroidery kits for her company, Wool & Hoop (woolandhoop. com). Her how-to book, *New Crewel* (2005), is published by Lark Books.

DIRECTIONS

What You'll Need: Medium-weight iron-on interfacing, T-shirt that fits you perfectly (I used white), Embroidery hoop (4 or 5 inches in diameter), Embroidery thread (the color of your tee)

1. Cut seven 1 1/2-inch circles out of iron-on interfacing.

2. Place your white T-shirt right-side up on an ironing board. Evenly space the interfacing circles, forming a row down the front center of your T-shirt. Make sure the bumpy iron-on stuff is facing down, toward the T-shirt. Carefully iron the circles onto the T-shirt. Avoid ironing with a back-and-forth motion, which will cause the circles to shift while you iron them down; instead, pick the iron up and place it down when you need to move from one circle to the next.

3. Using your embroidery hoop, hoop your T-shirt, starting with the bottom circle. Since your T-shirt is probably a stretchy, knit fabric, try not to pull the fabric too tight in the hoop, or your circles will become lopsided as you work.

4. Cut out a 1-inch circle from the center of the 1 1/2-inch, ironed-on, circle interfacings, leaving a 1/4-inch ring of interfacing with a 1-inch hole through the center of it and the tee underneath.

5. Next, cut a 20-inch length of embroidery floss and separate it into two 3-strand lengths. Thread your needle with one of the 3-strand lengths. Do not knot the end.

6. Stitch around the ring, making one straight, 1/4-inch stitch parallel to the next, one after the other, until you have gone all the way around the circle. Be careful to keep the tension the same on each stitch, not pulling too tightly or too loosely. Also, try to make the stitches close to each other without leaving any gaps, but without overlapping. What you are making is called an "eyelet hole."

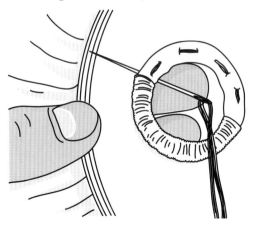

7. If you run out of thread and aren't quite finished with the circle, do not knot your thread. Instead, "tie off" your thread by taking your needle to the back of the design (inside the T-shirt) and weaving the needle through the existing stitches. Do this again in the opposite direction, and your thread should be secure. Cut the thread close so that no threads are hanging out. To start a new thread, do not make a knot at the end; simply weave the needle and thread through the existing stitches on the back side a couple of times in the opposite direction and then continue stitching on the front.

8. Repeat Steps 4 through 7 until you have finished all 7 eyelet holes, moving the embroidery hoop as you work.

9. Once you have finished stitching, give your T-shirt a quick press with a warm iron to get rid of any wrinkles.

Put on your creation, and wear it out to shock the town!

A NIFTY KNIT-TEE

by ★ Melissa Dettloff

DIFFICULTY LEVEL

L

100% COTTON
SEE REVERSE FOR CARE

I'm a pack rat—I keep everything, including every bit of scrap from the T-shirts I reconstruct—so I'm always trying to come up with new projects to put my leftovers to good use. One sleepless night, I thought, What if I knit a scarf with my T-shirt scraps? Why not?

As soon as I began working on my prototype, I found that I wasn't getting the results I was hoping for because the knitting needles I had weren't big enough. Anxious to finish the project, I looked around the house for larger substitutes. Rifling through a kitchen drawer, I came across two turkey basters—perfect!

Because most T-shirts are made of cotton, a natural fiber that retains warmth, the T-shirt scarf is soft and surprisingly warm. You'll be the only one on your block sporting this style, and they'll never guess how you made it.

A vintage Singer sewing machine, passed down from her late grandmother, sparked **Melissa Dettloff's** creative interests. Bored with post-collegiate working life, she created her own handmade clothing and accessory shop, Lekkner (lekkner. com). Melissa's specialty is reconstructing T-shirts: Send her a mass-produced T-shirt, and she'll turn it into a one-of-a-kind garment. Also, if she finds a reworkable tee at a local thrift shop, chances are it will also end up for sale on her site.

A strong believer in productive responsibility, Melissa donates a portion of Lekkner sales to animal-friendly organizations, Greyhound rescue in particular. Her pet project is Crafters for Critters (craftersforcritters.com), an annual fundraiser she organizes to raise money for animal-rescue programs across the country.

DIRECTIONS

What You'll Need: 5 T-shirts, Rotary blade, U.S. size 50 knitting needles or 2 turkey basters (seriously!), 2 skeins of yarn in a color that goes well with the tees

1. Start by cutting the bottom hem off each T-shirt. Next, cut the T-shirts vertically (from bottom to top) into 1-inch strips, trimming each strip before you hit the sleeves or neckline. To get the cleanest cuts with the least frustration, use a rotary blade and a ruler. This step takes a lot of time, so be prepared to chat on the phone or have friends over to help!

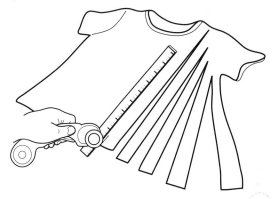

2. Once you've cut up all 5 T-shirts, you'll have a large pile of 1-inch wide strips. It's time to turn your pile of strips into one long strip—but first, mix up all the strips so you'll have random patterns in the scarf. Use a sewing machine (or, if you must, a needle and thread) to stitch together all the strips, end to end. I like to use a zigzag stitch, and then trim the excess for a neat finish. Don't forget to save a dozen strips for tassels! Once you've stitched all the pieces together, you'll have one long strip that will be the "yarn" for your scarf.

3. Now it's time to start your knittin' engines: using either large knitting needles or turkey basters, cast on 6 stitches. For extra texture and color, knit different yarns into your scarf along with the tee strip.

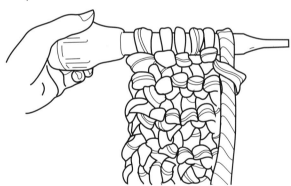

4. When the strip is nearly all knit, bind off and weave the ends into the scarf.

5. Knot the strips you set aside—along with some yarn—into tassels on the ends of the scarf.

Note: I used 5 average-sized T-shirts, which yielded a 67-yard strip. This strip made a scarf that is 2 1/3 yards long, not including tassels. My finished scarf is 6 stitches across and about 5 inches wide. You may want to use more or less fabric, depending on what size you'd like your scarf to be. Also, don't be afraid to experiment with stripes, polka dots, and screen-printed tees!

Now you're ready to face the weather in recycled style!

BUTTON-DOWN TEE

by ★ David Dalrymple with Patricia Field

DIFFICULTY LEVEL

L

100% COTTON

Sometimes crew-neck T-shirts can be a bit too casual, and the neck always seems to cut in and choke me; inevitably, I end up cutting out the neckline to show a bit more skin. Dress shirts sometimes seem a bit rigid and never seem to fit tight enough. Thus, the fusion of two classic styles—the T-shirt and the dress shirt. Get up in it!

Costume designer **Patricia Field** raised the standards for glamour with the groundbreaking fashion of *Sex and the City*. Her inimitable vision has earned her several honors, including two Emmy awards and the title of "Stylist of the Year" by the CFDA. Field's credits are varied and numerous. For more than 30 years, her Greenwich Village boutique has been a defining factor in the style of New York's glittery nightlife.

David Dalrymple, as head of design for Patricia Field's House of Field line from 1994 until 2004, created clothes for daring women as well as wardrobe pieces for HBO's *Sex and the City*. David's list of clients reads like a "who's who" of the music industry. Most notoriously, he designed the breakaway ensemble with which Britney Spears stopped the show at the 2000 MTV Music Awards.

DIRECTIONS

What You'll Need: Men's button-down shirt (a flannel, men's dress, or sport shirt, as long as it has a proper collar and buttons down the front), T-shirt with a snug, sexy fit

1. Grab the button-down shirt and use the scissors to cut out the front placket (the bit with the buttons, buttonholes, and collar). Starting on the side with the buttons, continue up, around the base of the collar, and down the side with the buttonholes. Cut about an inch away from the buttons, collar, and buttonholes, leaving a hefty bit of fabric for sewing. Make sure the button-down shirt's placket is longer than the front of your tee, from front collar to hem (most button-down shirts will be significantly longer than most tees).

2. Smooth your tee, right-side up, onto a large, flat work surface, and then pin the collar and the button side of the placket to the T-shirt. Button up the placket, and then line up the back of the button-down collar, where the shirt's tag is sewn, with the back of the tee collar, where that tag is sewn, fitting the button-down collar into the tee collar, so that the tee is on the outside, visible from behind.

3. Once you have the back and sides of the collars pinned together, smooth the buttoned placket onto the front of the T-shirt. Pin around the edge of the placket, leaving the raw edge of button-down-shirt fabric exposed. You can pin the placket straight down the front of the tee, or you can pin it askew, giving it a twisted, punk-rock look.

4. When you're finished with all that pinning, unbutton the buttons on the placket, leaving all the pins in place. Lift up the buttonhole side of the fabric, and you'll see a strip of tee tucked underneath, about a 1/2-inch wide. Carefully cut that strip of T-shirt, separating the 2 sides of the placket. Button the placket again—the tee should stay smooth.

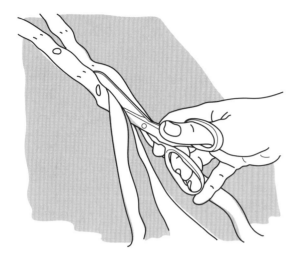

5. Time to get sewing! Use your sewing machine (or, if you must, a needle and thread) to stitch the placket and collar into place. Sew on both sides of the buttons and buttonholes—heck, go around twice for extra security! Trim off excess button-down-shirt fabric, leaving the edge raw so it can unravel a bit. Don't trim too close to your stitching!

6. Finally, cut off excess placket that extends longer than the tee. If you'd like, cut the bottom of your tee in the shape of the bottom of a dress shirt; it will roll up a little, but it will also give the look of a real dress shirt to your T-shirt.

Wear it open, showing a lot of chest.

PERPETUAL RECONSTRUCTION

by ★ Karly Hand

DIFFICULTY LEVEL

L

100% COTTON
SEE REVERSE FOR CARE

For this project, I didn't want to simply reconstruct a shirt; I wanted to highlight the art of reconstruction itself, to make a piece that was actually about reconstruction. I realized snap tape was a great way to create a T-shirt that could be recreated again and again.

When you cover a basic tee in snap tape, you create endless possibilities and combinations. I've provided a few examples, but the sky's the limit when it comes to new ways of gathering, snapping, and covering the shirt. Patches, buttons, lace, jewels, a photograph—you can sew almost anything to snap tape, adding or removing your embellishments whenever the urge strikes. I also added princess sleeves, which soften the snap tape's tough look, but you can fashion your sleeves any way you like: cut them off, keep them on, add sleeves from another top.

The best part about this project is that if you're not happy with your results, you can change them—in a snap!

Karly Hand put to work her art-school fascination with fabric and kinetics by creating her own line, Identity Crisis Clothing (identitycrisisclothing.com). Her dynamic designs often perform multiple functions or operate as more than one piece, keeping her challenged, motivated, and busy.

Karly loves her cat, Floyd, and thinks the ironic comeback of '80s hair bands is a slap in the face to true believers. A co-host of the DIY network's *Stylelicious*, Karly is also a member of the Austin Craft Mafia (austincraftmafia.com), a Texas-based collective of crafty ladies.

DIRECTIONS

What You'll Need: White T-shirt, Approximately 10 yards of white snap tape, Fabric dye in any color you like, Embellishments: zipper, fabric for ruffle (3 by 9 inches), silk flowers (all optional)

1. Since snap tape usually is only available in white, so you'll have to dye it to add color. Following the instructions on the package, dye the snap tape and T-shirt together. Once the tape and shirt are dry and the dye set, you're ready to start reconstruction.

2. Begin by cutting off your tee's sleeves, using the pre-existing armhole seams as a guide. Next, cut open the seam of each sleeve you just removed, so that you are left with two flat pieces of fabric. Cut off the sleeve edge just below the curve. Get ready to sew!

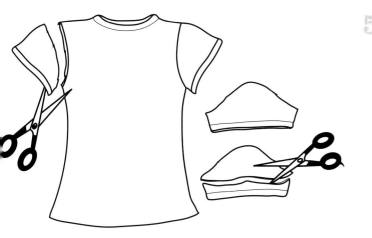

5. Do a little happy dance, because now comes the fun part—it's time to put on the snap tape! Starting at the bottom, left-hand corner of the shirt, fold in the edge at a 90-degree angle and press with an iron. Measure 2 1/2 inches from the fold you just pressed, fold again in the other direction, and press. Continue folding, accordion-style, until you have folded and pressed the entire shirt. Unfold the shirt.

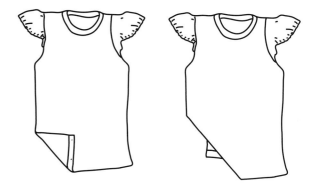

3. Using a sewing machine or needle and thread, baste the curved edge of the sleeves with an extra-long stitch; be careful not to backstitch the ends—you'll need them loose to make the gather. Pull the bottom thread of the basted stitch to gather the edge of the sleeve and create a ruffle.

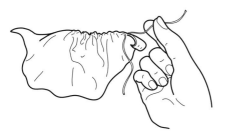

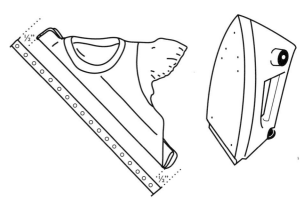

4. With right sides together, pin the sleeves back on the shirt. Carefully stitch the gathered sleeves back on the shirt using a standard stitch.

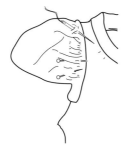

6. Using the folds as a guide, cut strips of "outie" side of the snap tape 1 inch longer than the length of each fold so that there is a 1/2 inch of tape at each end to tuck under and sew.

7. Pin the snap tape to each fold. Fold the raw edges of the tape under and stitch along the edges of the tape. Repeat until all front and back folds are covered.

Now that you have the basic shirt down, it's time to personalize! You can use the "innie" side of the snap tape to wrap around, gather, and snap the shirt, and you can also add accessories. I've included instructions for attaching a few festive items, but feel free to let your own imagination guide you.

To Add a Zipper:

1. Cut 2 pieces of snap tape the same length as your zipper. This time, use the "innie" side (the opposite side from that "outie" side, which is on the shirt).

2. Pin the tape to the zipper, making sure that the working side of the snap faces the opposite direction from the working part of the zipper. Stitch the snap tape to the zipper.

To Add Flowers:

1. Remove the heads of silk flowers from the stems and any other plastic parts.

2. Cut a piece of snap tape with 2 snaps on it. Pin the flower in the center between the 2 snaps, and then stitch it in place using a zigzag stitch.

LOST IN
AUSTIN

I'm the farthest thing from a "T-shirt and jeans" person. I don't wear pants, for one thing; for another, those straight, boy-cut T-shirts look terrible on me. Here's a nice way to femme-up any T-shirt so that even I would wear it. If you're new to crochet, pick up a beginner's book or look online for the basics. Crochet can sound confusing, but once you understand the basics, it's really a breeze.

You can wear the end result with a circle skirt and cowboy boots for a nice country feel, a denim skirt and clogs for a more Scandinavian look, or yes, even a pair of jeans. I worked up this sample on a train from Austin to Chicago, which is how it got its name.

Debbie Stoller, an outspoken feminist all her life, has also been, for many of those years, a closet crafter. In 1993 she co-founded *BUST* magazine (bust.com), where she serves as co-publisher and editor-in-chief.

In 2003, she went public with her needle-wielding ways and published *Stitch 'N Bitch: The Knitter's Handbook* (Workman, 2003), which was followed in 2004 by *Stitch 'N Bitch Nation* (Workman) and in 2006 by *Stitch 'N Bitch Crochet: The Happy Hooker* (Workman). She lives in Brooklyn, where she likes to sew, embroider, knit, crochet, garden, bird-watch, and engage in a wide variety of other geeky activities.

DIRECTIONS

What You'll Need: T-shirt that fits to your liking, 1 ball 100% mercerized Paton's Grace or any other sport-weight yarn (choose a color to match your T-shirt), 36-inch piece of 3/16-inch-wide ribbon in matching or contrasting color, Size D crochet hook, Tapestry needle (the thinnest you can find that you can still thread the yarn through)

✳   ✳   ✳

Making the Sleeve Edging:

1. Smooth your tee on a flat surface. Using tailor's chalk, make a dot on the sleeve along the top edge, 5 inches out from the seam at the shoulder, and a second dot 4 inches out from the seam at the armpit. Connect the dots, and then cut along the line. Repeat on other sleeve.

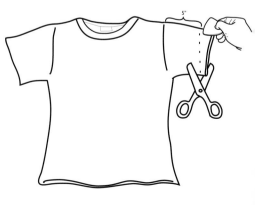

2. Thread an 18-inch piece of yarn through your needle. Beginning at the armpit edge of your tee, fold the cut sleeve edge about 3/8 inch (just under 1/4 inch) to the inside, and make blanket stitches along the edge to hold down the hem. Each stitch should be about 1/4 inch deep and 1/4 inch apart—this small size is important.

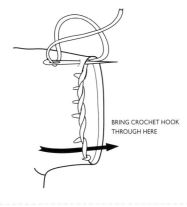

BRING CROCHET HOOK THROUGH HERE

3. Now it's time to start your crocheting engines!

Row 1: Place a slipknot on your crochet hook, and beginning at the armpit edge, make a single crochet into the bottom of the 1st blanket stitch (the strand that runs along the edge of your hem). Chain 1. Single crochet into the next blanket stitch, and then chain 1. Continue making single-crochet stitches into the blanket stitch, followed by a chain 1, until you reach your original single crochet. Slipstitch into the top of that stitch.

Row 2: Chain 5, and then skip 2 stitches and double crochet into the 3rd stitch, making sure that you insert your hook under the top 2 strands of that stitch. Chain 2. Skip the next 2 stitches, double crochet into the stitch after that, and then chain 2. Continue in this manner all the way around the sleeve, making sure to always insert your hook under at least 2 strands of the stitch you are crocheting into, whether it's a single crochet or a chain stitch in the row below. When you get to the end of the row, you may have only 1 stitch to skip instead of 2—don't worry about it. Just make your final double crochet, chain 2, and then end the round by making a slipknot in the 3rd chain of the turning chain. It's really not as complicated as it sounds!

Row 3: Chain 5, skip 2 stitches, and then double crochet into the top of the next double-crochet stitch. Chain 2, double crochet into the top of the next double-crochet stitch, and then continue in this way until you complete the round. Slipstitch into the top of the 1st double crochet.

Row 4: Chain 3, make 2 double crochets into the 1st chain space, and then single crochet into next chain space. Make 5 double crochets into the next chain space, and then single crochet into the next chain space. Repeat these 2 steps (5 double crochets into next chain-2 space, single crochet into next chain-2 space) all the way around. Double crochet into first chain-2 space, and then slipstitch into the top of the turning chain to end the round. Finish off yarn.

4. Beginning at the top of the shoulder, weave an 8-inch-long piece of ribbon through Row 2. Tie it in a knot or bow, either gathering in the sleeve or leaving it loose, however you like. Trim the ribbon to your preferred length.

5. Repeat all steps for the other sleeve.

Making the Neck Edging:

1. Smooth your tee on a flat work surface. Using tailor's chalk, mark a dot about 3 inches down from the lowest point of the T-shirt collar, and make 2 dots along the shoulder, 4 inches straight out to the right and the left of the T-shirt collar. Connect these 3 dots with a curved line to create a guide for cutting out a shallow scoop neck. Carefully cut out the front neckline, following the line you just drew. Then, using the new neckline as a guide, mark a parallel line across the inside back of the T-shirt, about 1 inch shallower at its center point than the front. Cut along the line.

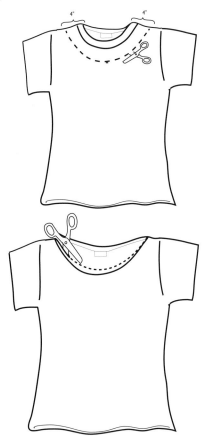

2. Hem the neckline as you did in Step 2 above, using blanket stitches 1/4 inch deep and spaced 1/4 inch apart.

3. Get out your crochet hook again.

Row 1: Same as for sleeve edging, above: Place a slipknot on your crochet hook, and beginning at the armpit edge, make a single crochet into the bottom of the 1st blanket stitch (the strand that runs along the edge of your hem). Chain 1. Single crochet into the next blanket stitch, and then chain 1. Continue making single-crochet stitches into the blanket stitch, followed by a chain 1, until you reach your original single crochet. Slipstitch into the top of that stitch.

Row 2: Chain 5, and then skip 3 stitches and double crochet into the 3rd stitch, making sure that you insert your hook under the top 2 strands of that stitch. Chain 2. Skip the next 3 stitches, double crochet into the next stitch, and then chain 2. Continue in this manner all the way around. When you get to the end, you may have only 1 or 2 stitches to skip instead of 3; don't worry about it. Just make your final double crochet, chain 2, and then end the round by making a slipknot in the 3rd chain of the turning chain.

Row 3: Chain 5, skip 2 stitches, and then double crochet into the top of the next double-crochet stitch. Chain 1, double crochet into the top of the next-double crochet stitch, chain 2, and then double crochet into the top of the next double-crochet stitch. Continue in this way—alternating chain 1 and chain 2 between double-crochet stitches—until you complete the round. Slipstitch into the top of the 1st double crochet.

Row 4: Same as for sleeve edging, above: Chain 3, make 2 double crochets into the 1st chain space, and then single crochet into next chain space. Make 5 double crochets into the next chain space, and then single crochet into the next chain space. Repeat these 2 steps (5 double crochets into next chain-2 space, single crochet into next chain-2 space) all the way around. Double crochet into first chain-2 space, and then slipstitch into the top of the turning chain to end the round. Finish off yarn.

4. Beginning at the center of the front, weave a 24-inch-long piece of ribbon through Row 2. Tie in a small bow at front. Trim ribbon to your preferred length.

Slip on your stylie little tee, and see if you can't get yourself lost in Austin.

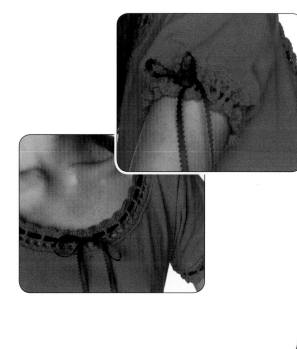

I've been reworking clothes since childhood. In fact, I learned to hand-sew by cutting up or adding to existing clothing to create new pieces. Two years ago, my boyfriend gave me a serger for Christmas, and I started working with knits. By incorporating knits into T-shirt redesign, I discovered a new way to produce more flattering tees, which is how the Toga Tee came about.

I love combining a wide variety of colors and graphics to create something beautiful, cool, and comfortable out of something ugly or unflattering, and this project is a great chance to do just that. There are always tons of T-shirts at thrift stores, and they needn't be pretty at the outset to be fabulous in the future.

Tying up one sleeve with a ribbon is a detail I borrowed from my sister, who'd done it with one of her tees. Needless to say, I thought it looked pretty cool, too!

Chia Guillory is probably most well known for her unique faux-fur CHIAHATS (chiahats.com). She also designs and sews a variety of accessories and seasonal clothing lines.

Chia is a self-taught designer who, since childhood, has had an obsession with clothing from many eras. At a young age, she began hand-sewing Victorian-inspired clothing and hats for her vintage dolls. As an adult, Chia still finds inspiration from vintage styles, also drawing her ideas from traditional, indigenous clothing, nature, art, and her family.

As an artist who creates everything from found-object sculpture to elaborate figure drawings, Chia finds that her clothing designs and artwork often intermingle, making her clothing lines very interesting and definitely one-of-a-kind.

DIRECTIONS

What You'll Need: Measuring tape, 2 oversized T-shirts (coordinated colors), Snug-fitting tank top (one you already own), 30-inch length of 1/2-inch wide ribbon

1. Using the measuring tape, measure around your bust line. Divide the measurement by 4 and write it down. For example, if your bust is 36 inches, write down "9 inches."

2. To find the vertical center of your T-shirt, fold it in half, matching sleeve to sleeve. Using the measuring tape, measure the number of inches you wrote down in Step 1 out from the center at the bust line, and mark it with chalk. Do the same for the other side of the shirt. Open up the shirt, and you'll have 2 marks, showing the width of your bust line.

3. Now you're going to use your tank top to create a pattern on your oversized tee. Turn your T-shirt inside out and smooth it flat on your worktable. Lay the tank top on the tee, so that the bottom curves of the tank's armholes match up with your chalk marks. Using tailor's chalk, trace the shape of the tank top onto your T-shirt.

4. Lift the tank top off your T-shirt. Finish drawing your chalk pattern by making the neck line a shallow scoop, curving the bottom of the shirt, and tapering in at the waist.

5. Now that you have your pattern, pin the front and back layers of the T-shirt together, and then cut on the chalk line through both layers of the shirt.

6. Using a sewing machine (or needle and thread, if you must), stitch together the two sides of tee at the top and sides, leaving a 1/4-inch seam allowance. (Look at you go! Way to sew!)

7. Next you'll be making your new, contrasting sleeves. Start by cutting along the seam line to remove the sleeves of your 2nd T-shirt. Slice the sleeves open and lay them flat. Using tailor's chalk, mark the flattened sleeve's vertical middle at the factory-stitched hemline.

8. Decide on the appropriate length for your new sleeve; I recommend 3 to 6 inches. Mark that length on the flat T-shirt sleeve, in line with the middle mark. We'll call this the Shoulder Mark (as opposed to the more popular Marky Mark).

9. Using the measuring tape, measure around your upper arm at the place where your sleeve will end. For comfort, add 1 inch to this number. Now divide that number by 2, and write it down. For example, if your arm is 7 inches around, add 1 inch to make it 8 inches, and then divide by 2 to get 4 inches.

10. Now measure that number (4 inches in my example) out from the center mark to the left and mark it, then repeat to the right. At those marks, draw a 2-inch-long vertical line. We'll call this the Underarm Seam (because, really, why not?).

11. Draw a gentle, S-shaped line from the Shoulder Mark to the top of the Underarm Seam. Repeat on the other side to create a smooth, hump-shaped pattern. Cut along the pattern. Lay the cut sleeve on the second sleeve, trace the pattern, and cut out your second sleeve.

12. Pin the Underarm Seams (right sides) together to create a new sleeve. Repeat on the second sleeve.

13. Attach the sleeves to the shirt by pinning the right side of the sleeve to the right side of the shirt at the Underarm Seam and the shirt's side seam. Sew on the sleeve, and repeat on the other side.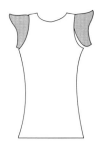

14. For your fancy final embellishment, sew a piece of ribbon inside the shirt at the shoulder seam. Thread one end of the ribbon up through the neckline and the other end through the sleeve. Bring the ends of the ribbon together and tie them into a bow at your shoulder—so cute!

Now go get 'em, Tiger!

BEACHY TUNIC

My fascination with T-shirts started in junior high, when I learned screen-printing to make my own tees. I got into making satirical and political tees, and then moved on to making bootleg commemorative tees to sell at Clash concerts and other events. I began to collect T-shirts for their prints or messages, and I would print on top of whatever was there, like a collage. Often, I didn't like the cut of a shirt, so I had to tailor them for the fit I wanted.

Today I do the same, except now I sell my creations in stores. I still like to pass along recycled tees, so I get leftover T-shirts from my little nephews and seconds from mills, and I take them apart and put them together again. I'm a print designer, and the print on the shirt shown here is one of my own, but you can make this beachy tunic from any T-shirt you love.

Liza Niles, born in Kalamazoo, Michigan, grew up in Philadelphia, studied fiber and textile design in Boston, and then lived in New York City, where she designed prints for J.Crew, American Eagle Outfitters, Tommy Hilfiger, and Nautica. At the same time, Liza was an adjunct teacher at Parsons School of Design in the textile and computer departments, and a consultant for the textile software company Pointcarre.

Eager to work with sustainable textiles, Liza now works with development organizations and schools that support craft and design, while collaborating with local artisans. She has studied and worked as a designer-in-residence in West Africa, the Dominican Republic, India, South America, and Japan. Liza now lives and works in Mexico City.

DIRECTIONS

What You'll Need: Oversized T-shirt, Shirt that fits you perfectly (to copy shape), Safety pins

1. Start by cutting off the bottom hem of your oversized T-shirt. Set the hem aside, but keep track of it because you'll need it later. Next, smooth the shirt on a flat work surface. Turn the perfect-fit T-shirt inside out, and then place it on top of the larger shirt. Using tailor's chalk, trace the shape of the neck, sleeves, and sides (but not the bottom) of the perfect-fit tee onto the large shirt. Remove your well-fitting tee and return it to your T-shirt drawer. Cut along your chalk outline, through both layers of fabric. The original seams on the oversized tee should now be open along the body, but the shirt will still be full-length.

2. Using tailor's chalk, draw a new, scooped neckline onto the oversized tee. The front neckline should scoop lower than the back; your neckline can be freeform—it's a beachy tunic, after all! If the sleeves are too big and boxy, draw on the sleeve shape you like. Cut along the chalk line at the neck and sleeves, and then trim the hems off the sleeves.

3. Separate the front and back pieces of your tee, and then match them up so that the right sides are facing. Pin along the shoulders and sides, and then sew the shirt back together again, using a 1/4-inch seam allowance. Leave the last couple of inches on the side seam open, as I did, for a breezy, show-off-your-legs look. Ooh la la!

4. To make the gathered pull (also known as a "ruche") that gives the tunic its bikini-worthy shape, find the reinforced neckline material that you cut off the shirt body earlier. From this piece, cut a 10-inch piece and carefully trim it to about 1/4 inch away from the

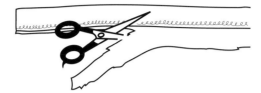

seam. With the shirt still inside out, pin this piece, centered along one of shirt's side seams, lining up one open end of the neckline material to the bottom of the seam. Leave the two ends of the attached piece open, which creates a kind of tunnel. Sew the piece in place along on both sides of the length, where it's pinned.

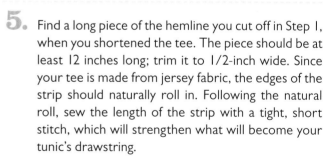

5. Find a long piece of the hemline you cut off in Step 1, when you shortened the tee. The piece should be at least 12 inches long; trim it to 1/2-inch wide. Since your tee is made from jersey fabric, the edges of the strip should naturally roll in. Following the natural roll, sew the length of the strip with a tight, short stitch, which will strengthen what will become your tunic's drawstring.

6. Attach a medium-sized safety pin to one end of the drawstring. Thread the safety pin into the bottom of the sewn "tunnel," on the inside of the shirt, and work it through until a 1/2 inch comes through on the top of the panel. Make sure the string lies flat inside the panel, and then sew along the top of the panel, widthwise, so that you sew over the inserted drawstring. This will keep the string in place when you tie it. The excess at the top of the drawstring can be trimmed off; you should have about 1 1/2 inch of the drawstring left over at the bottom end. Make a large knot in the drawstring at this end.

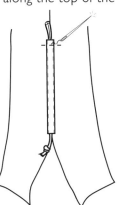

7. Turn the shirt right-side out again, and gently pull the new drawstring. As you do this, the shirt will scrunch up, so pull the drawstring to create the amount of "scrunchiness" that you want.

Now you're ready for the disco and the beach— in the same day. Your handmade tunic is super- sexy and original, just like you!

Start with a phrase that's been knocking around in your head, and let your imagination run wild—don't be afraid to spice up your phrase or change it a bit! Taking a cue from artist Jenny Holzer, I found a use for this odd quote from our local newspaper, which I'd been saving for just such an occasion.

Since my medium is cross-stitch, and it would be more than tricky to cross-stitch on a T-shirt, I opted to use cross-stitch material in a band. Of course, I'm so mad for pom-pom fringe that I would have made solid cha-cha sleeves if I'd had time. Let your own muse direct you—go all out, and create a T-shirt that expresses your own insani-tee.

Julie Jackson was not cut out for the rat race. Dealing with an idiot boss led her to find solace in picking up a hobby from fifth grade and updating it with passive-aggressive phrases. At first it was just good therapy, but soon Subversive Cross Stitch (subversivecrossstitch.com) became an internet sensation and Julie began selling cross stitch kits of her patterns.

Within a year, her kits were selling across America. Her work has been seen in magazines and galleries worldwide and has been described as "the cross-stitch version of rap music." Her book, *Subversive Cross Stitch: 33 Patterns for Your Surly Side* (2006) is published by Chronicle Books. Julie lives in Dallas with her charming husband and menagerie of pets.

DIRECTIONS

What You'll Need: T-shirt, Long strip of cross-stitch fabric in ribbon form, Embroidery needle, Embroidery floss in color(s) of your choice, Interfacing, Various trim: pom-pom fringe, ruffles, ribbon—whatever floats your boat

1. Start by washing the cross-stitch ribbon and T-shirt to make sure they won't shrink later. Think about how you would like to lay out your words on your shirt: in one row across the front, in bits and pieces all over the front of the shirt, or whatever appeals to your particular sense of whimsy.

2. Using embroidery floss and an embroidery needle, cross-stitch your phrase onto the ribbon of cross-stitch fabric. You might need to leave extra space between words for cutting, depending on how you decide to lay out the phrase on your shirt.

Note: *If you don't know the ins and outs of cross stitching, you can find animated instructions at my site, subversivecrossstitch.com.*

3. On a flat work surface, lay the tee face up, and cut out a square neckline.

4. Turn the shirt inside out, iron interfacing around the neckline to reinforce it, and then trim off the excess interfacing.

5. Turn the shirt right-side out. Place the trim along the neckline, pin it in place, and then sew it down using a standard stitch. Repeat these steps for the sleeves.

6. Now for the cross-stitched band. (Strike up the band!) Iron interfacing to the back of each piece of cross-stitched material, which will ensure the thread ends stay put and don't eventually work their way out of the material in front.

7. Cut the band as appropriate and pin it into place. Using a needle and thread, sew each section onto your tee.

Now you have a charming and alarming tee!

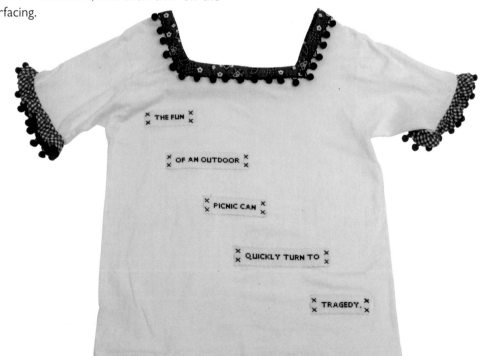

Here's a neat way to turn a plain, boxy T-shirt into a curve-flattering top with puff sleeves and sparkly vintage trim. The retro-styled pin tucks create a very feminine line in eye-catching contrast colors, and they're easy to make with straight pins and a sewing machine.

I used two shades of pink thread (one on the spool and one in the bobbin) on a black shirt for a shimmery effect. Mix lights and darks or use the same color as your fabric—it's up to you!

For a sleeker line, use the same pin-tucking technique, but on the inside of the shirt (just turn the shirt inside out before completing the pin-tucking instructions). When you turn the shirt right-side out, the pin-tucked lines will look smooth and subtle, but still define the shaping.

Why be plain and boxy when you can be cute and curvy?

Susan Beal is a writer and crafter who lives in Portland, Oregon, and Los Angeles, California. Her handmade jewelry line, susanstars (susanstars.com), is sold online and in shops and galleries across the country. She loves thrift-store shopping, sewing, and cupcakes (not necessarily in that order).

Susan writes about art, craft, and fashion for getcrafty.com, *BUST, Venus,* and *ReadyMade.* Her first book, *Super Crafty: 75 Amazing How-to Projects* (2005), co-written with her fellow craft superheroes of PDX Super Crafty (pdxsupercrafty.com), was published by Sasquatch Books.

DIRECTIONS

What You'll Need: Boxy T-shirt in your size or 1 size bigger, Sewing machine with ballpoint needle, 2/3 yard of 3/8-inch wide elastic, Elastic guide or large safety pin, 2 yards of vintage or new trim or lace (with a little stretch

1. Pin a neat, vertical crease in the fabric of the T-shirt, starting at the left shoulder. The pinheads should be angled out to the left side, with the sharp points facing the center of the shirt. The pin-tuck fold line will follow the slight curve of the shoulder seam and should measure about 7 inches from top to bottom.

2. Repeat to form 3 more pin tucks, spaced 1 inch apart, at the top of the shirt. The pin tucks should be parallel at the top and angled diagonally at the bottom.

3. Create 4 more pin tucks on the right side of the shirt, symmetrical with the left side, pinheads facing out and points facing the center—for safety's sake!

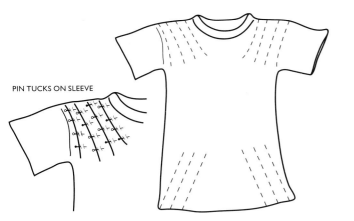

PIN TUCKS ON SLEEVE

4. Using a long stitch length, sew the 1st (outer) pin tuck at the left shoulder. Stitch from the bottom to the top, backstitching at the beginning and the end to hold the seam. The pin tuck should be approximately 1/4-inch wide.

5. Sew the next 3 pin tucks on the left side in the same way, working from left to right, so the inner pin tuck is the last one you create.

6. Now you'll sew the pin tucks on the right side. Start with the outer pin tuck, stitching from top to bottom this time. Repeat to sew the other 3 pin tucks, working from right to left, so the inner fold is the last one you sew. Things are starting to look curvier!

7. Pin 3 diagonal creases at the bottom of the left side of the shirt, spaced about 1 1/2 inches apart, that measure 10 inches long.

8. Pin 3 diagonal creases at the bottom of the right side of the shirt, so they are symmetrical with the left side.

9. Stitch the 1st, outer pin tuck on the left side from the bottom to the top. Backstitch at the beginning and end of the seam. Sew the next 2 pin tucks on the left side the same way, working from left to right.

10. Sew the pin tucks on the right side in the same way, starting with the outer pin tuck and stitching from top to bottom on each one.

11. Trim the excess thread from all pin tuck seams, and the hard part is done!

To Make the Sleeves Cute 'n' Curvy:

1. Cut the elastic into two 10-inch pieces. Cut a small slit on either side of the seam at the bottom inside of the sleeve. Look at the illustration for clarification—this step might sound a little tricky, but it's really not.

ELASTIC IN SLEEVE

2. Thread one end of the elastic into an elastic guide (or pin a large safety pin to one end of the elastic). Guide the elastic through one of the openings you made in the previous step, and pull it all the way around the sleeve, and out through the other opening. Pin the elastic to hold it in place, gathering the fabric evenly for a puffed effect. Take a minute to ponder the miracle of elastic guides and wonder where we'd be without them. Repeat on the other sleeve. Be sure to try on the shirt to make sure the elastic is comfortable.

3. Hand-sew or machine-stitch the ends of the elastic together to secure them, first making sure it isn't twisted. Trim the ends of the elastic.

4. Hand-sew or machine-stitch the opening closed on both sleeves. Now you have poofy fun!

Embellishments:

1. Starting at the back, pin trim or lace around the collar, letting it overlap slightly. Make sure the trim has enough stretch so that the shirt will still go over your head (this should be obvious, but you'd be surprised). I used 20 inches of trim to decorate my collar. Machine-stitch the trim, using a long stitch length, and backstitch to end the seam.

2. Starting at one side, pin trim around the hem of the T-shirt, overlapping it the same way as you did with the collar. Make sure the pin tucks are all lying smoothly and facing the sides under the trim. Machine-stitch around the trim in the same way as you did the collar.

Time to celebrate your success—put it on and do a sassy little dance, curvy lady!

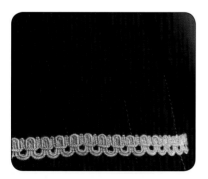

SOFT-TEE BOX

by ★ Stephanie Wenzel

DIFFICULTY LEVEL

L

100% COTTON
SEE REVERSE FOR CARE

Here at the SWIGG compound, any empty space is quickly overtaken by boxes—shipping boxes, packing boxes, storage boxes, tall boxes, small boxes, short boxes, long boxes. But unlike the fish from your favorite Dr. Seuss book, these boxes are not red or blue—they are all one color...brown.

Now, I love brown—a rich, dark, fudgy brown the color of Valhrona chocolate bars, deep walnut-stained modern furniture, and fierce grizzlies—but being surrounded by corrugated-box brown, which blends in with our dust-bowl brown floors, makes me feel like I'm working in a dry, arid brushland, with no clouds, no shade, and no chance of taking a swim in a lake anytime soon. I decided to take those grapes and make them into wine, take what's old and make it gold, take your daily frock and make it rock!

The opportunity to reinvent these desert surroundings into a colorful, voluptuous, ethereal landscape of T-shirt-ous desire was no mirage...behold the soft-tee box!

Stephanie Wenzel, a graphic artist living and working in Brooklyn, New York, is the founder of SWIGG Studio (thisisswigg.com), a multi-disciplined design firm, and SWIGG Products, tactile goods for human enjoyment.

Her website won an Interactive Design Award from *HOW* magazine in 2005, and her work has been seen internationally in the "Neighbourhood" exhibition at the Pictoplasma Conference in Berlin, the Sneaker Pimps world tour, and the Riviera Gallery in Brooklyn, as well as in the graphic-design publications *Novum* and *Items*.

DIRECTIONS

What You'll Need: T-shirt sized youth large, Seam ripper or X-Acto blade, Rotary cutter, 16-by-20-inch piece of chipboard or mat board, cut to 2 pieces each that measure 3-by-5, 3-by-7, and 5-by-7 inches, 45-by-60-inch roll of hi-loft batting (cut to 6 pieces each that measure 3-by-5, 3-by-7, and 5-by-7 inches), High-tack spray adhesive

1. Turn your T-shirt inside out. Using a seam ripper or X-Acto blade, remove the looped tag from the T-shirt collar, being careful not to rip or cut into it. Take this tag and cut it into 2 separate, but equal, pieces. Save 1 of the pieces, which will be used for the tab on your finished box, and toss the other. (If your tag wasn't looped, but just one of those cheapo, white, 1-ply tags, you'll just use that, intact, for your tab.)

2. Smooth your T-shirt onto a flat work surface, face up, still inside out. Using a rotary cutter, trim off the sleeves and collar, and then discard them. Then, using your straightedge ruler, trim off the hem at the bottom of the T-shirt and set it aside to use later. Trim as straight as possible without cutting into the stitching of the hem.

3. Your tee should still be inside out, spread flat on the table. If your T-shirt has graphics on it that you want to appear on the outside of the box, flip the shirt over so that this piece is on the bottom (still inside out). Iron your pieces in preparation for accurate cutting. Photocopy the nifty template I included, increasing it by 528%.

4. Pin the pattern to your tee fabric, going through both layers of fabric. Using your rotary cutter and straightedge ruler, cut around the template. If you use a youth large T-shirt or larger, the template will fit vertically on your 2 pieces.

5. Once your pieces are cut, re-pin them together, placing the pins 1/4 inch away from the edge, as shown. Find the tag you saved in Step 1, and then insert it, face down, in between the pieces at the top of the template. The cut edge of the tag should face out.

6. Sew the pieces together, leaving a 1/4-inch seam allowance. Start and stop at the spots indicated on the diagram to the right, which will leave you about a 6-inch opening on one of the 9-inch sides. Once finished, cut off the exterior corners at a 90-degree angle, and then cut a slit in the inner corners, which will eliminate bunching and pinching when your box is right-side out. This is your box cover. Turn the box cover right-side out, iron it flat, and set it aside.

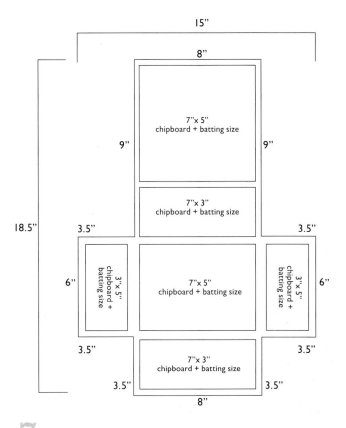

15"

8"

7"x 5"
chipboard + batting size

9"   9"

7"x 3"
chipboard + batting size

18.5"   3.5"   3.5"

6"

3"x 5"
chipboard + batting size

7"x 5"
chipboard + batting size

3"x 5"
chipboard + batting size

6"

3.5"   3.5"

7"x 3"
chipboard + batting size

3.5"   3.5"

8"

7. If you haven't cut your chipboard and batting, do it now. If you've already cut it, get yourself a nice, cool glass of water.

8. On each piece of board, use high-tack spray adhesive to attach 2 pieces of batting on the bottom side and 1 piece of batting on the top side. Be sure to secure the batting to the board along the edges and corners, as you want as little board exposed as possible. This lovely batting will ensure your box is soft and springy.

9. One at a time, insert the batting-covered box sides into the box cover through the 6-inch opening. Make sure the double layers of batting are facing down, touching the part of the box cover that you intend to be the outside of your box. Stuff the pieces in place according to the original diagram. Start with a 3-by-7-inch side, insert the two 3-by-5-inch sides, then the first 5-by-7-inch, then the second 3-by-7-inch, and then the last 5-by-7-inch. Leave some wiggle room between all the pieces, so that you can fold up the sides easily. Also be sure that the batting is nice and flat once the pieces are inserted. Sometimes the adhesive will not hold the batting to the corners adequately, so if you have to, use your fingers to push any bunched batting into the corners. Finally, use a needle and thread to stitch up the 6-inch opening.

10. Take the hem of the T-shirt, which you cut off and set aside in Step 2, and cut the loop at I of the seams, creating one long strip of hem. Make sure the hem strip looks nice and even and pretty, trimming any stray bits. Fold up the sides of the box and wrap the hem strip around the 4 vertical sides of the box (see diagram). Secure the hem strip with a knot in the front of the box, and then trim off any excess. Fold down the top of the box to close it. Initially, keep pushing the top down, so that it fits snugly between the 4 vertical sides. After a few days, the top will sit naturally on its own.

11. Accessorize your Soft-Tee Box by sticking your favorite pins in the fluffy sides, or decorate the box with anything else that strikes your fancy.

Inside your Soft-Tee Box, you'll have plenty of room to store all your friendship bracelets and notes from your secret admirers!

ELASTICI-TEE

by ★ Susann Keohane

DIFFICULTY LEVEL

M

100% COTTON
SEE REVERSE FOR CARE

When everything in your closet looks drab, this T-shirt revamp is quick and easy to stitch. Wear it with jeans, and you have a sassy new outfit. You have complete control of the finished product's length—depending on how much you stretch the elastic when you sew it in place, you could end up with a midriff-baring number or a long, ruffly tunic.

Susann's love for everything handmade started at a young age. Her older relatives knitted beautiful afghans that sparked Susann's creative interests. She expressed her individuality by creating her own clothes and modeling them in (family–only!) mini–fashion shows.

Curious about the way clothes were constructed, she soon learned how to sew, sharpening her skills through years of creating costumes and fashions for friends. In 2003, a happy accident of selling a skirt that she'd made too small led her to establish her own clothing company and online boutique, All Dressed Up and Shy (alldressedupandshy.com).

A co-host on the DIY network's *Stylicious*, Susann is also a member of the Austin Craft Mafia (austincraftmafia.com), a Texas-based collective of crafty ladies.

DIRECTIONS

What You'll Need: Well-fitting T-shirt, Serger (if available), 1 yard of 3/8-inch elastic

1. Start with a comfy T-shirt and then break out the scissors! Cut out the neck hem and the bottom hem.

2. To create cap sleeves, cut a straight line up the sleeve, beginning at the inner bottom of the sleeve and cutting upward at an angle. Slice through both layers of fabric.

3. If you happen to have a serger, serge all newly created raw edges. If not, don't worry about it—this step isn't essential, but it adds a professional touch.

4. Turn the shirt inside out. On the inside front of the shirt, use the tailor's chalk and ruler to draw 2 straight lines, each beginning 1 inch in from the neck edge and ending at the waist hem.

5. Cut 2 pieces of elastic that are 2 inches longer than the length of your shirt.

6. Pin 1 piece of elastic loosely along the pencil line, just to hold it in place.

7. Starting at the top of the shirt, stitch the elastic to the T-shirt. Pull the elastic as you sew to create a gather. Remember, the length of your shirt will depend on how much you stretch the elastic as you sew it, so take it easy with the elastic unless you want a teeny belly shirt!

8. Repeat Steps 6 and 7 on the second line.

9. Turn the shirt right-side out, and you have a sassy new tee!

CAR-LOT
HANGING BANNERS

by ★ Jenny Mitchell

DIFFICULTY LEVEL

S

100% COTTON
SEE REVERSE FOR CARE

I'd been hanging onto a small stash of T-shirts for a while, just waiting for the right project to come along. One day, I had a brainstorm to transform all those leftover tees in a decorative room banner. This project is a great way to recycle, clean out your dresser drawer, and add a splash of color to an otherwise boring room, all at once!

You can work with as many different T-shirts as you want, depending on how colorful and patterned you want your flag to be. The more tees you use, the more T-shirt material you have, the longer your banner can be…get the picture? Use this flag banner for a summer BBQ, a kid's room decoration, or strung across your porch to announce a special occasion. ("Happy Arbor Day!")

It's easy to add your own special touches and make your banner stand out. Stencil a name, a message, or an image onto solid-colored T-shirts, or go all out and use as many different patterns and colors as you want. Add buttons, rickrack, pom-poms…gosh, the possibilities are almost endless!

Jenny Mitchell founded Frecklewonder (frecklewonder.com) in the summer of 2003. It's a fun mix of Jenny's handmade creations and favorite vintage finds—there's a little something for everyone.

Since Jenny strongly believes in being unique on a budget, she does her best to sell small-batch and one-of-a-kind items at affordable prices. Her tech-savvy hubby, Matt, helps with the behind-the-scenes website stuff, and her cute 4-year-old son, Henry, occasionally lends a hand in the modeling department.

On the heels of being chosen as one of fredflare.com's "Next Big Thing" sites in the spring of 2005, Jenny expanded her handmade line to include clothing inspired by her collection of 1960s fashion patterns.

DIRECTIONS

What You'll Need: Cardstock-weight paper, T-shirts (approximately 4 flags per shirt), 1-2 yards of lightweight interfacing, Cotton clothesline (or similar) rope

1. On cardstock, use a pencil and ruler to draw a triangle that you'll use as a template. My template was 7 inches long on each side, but you could make yours bigger or smaller. Cut out your template and set it somewhere safe.

2. Ready your tees for their transformation into flags. Remove the neck and sleeves of each T-shirt, so that you're left with the rectangular body part of each tee. Cut off the side seams so that you have two large rectangles of fabric. You won't be using the sleeves or the cut-off seams, so you can discard them or stash them away for another project.

3. T-shirt material is slippery and can be difficult to work with, so simplify your life (and this project) by ironing fusible interfacing onto the back side of each rectangle, covering it completely and trimming any edges. Yes, you'll be using a lot of interfacing for this project, but it's cheap and worth it!

4. Once all your T-shirt rectangles are interfaced, you'll need the triangle template you made in Step 1. Turn over the interfaced fabric so that the interfacing side is up. Use tailor's chalk to trace as many triangle shapes as you can fit onto the fabric—you should be able to get at least 4 triangles from each rectangle, depending upon the size of your templates and shirts. Repeat for each piece of interfaced fabric. Carefully cut out all your triangles, discarding the scraps.

5. The next step is best explained using the Pizza Analogy. Imagine that each flag is made up of 2 pieces of pizza. Match up the crusts for the top part of the flag, where it will attach to the rope. The "saucy topping parts" (the pattern/right sides of the T-shirt)

will face out, and the "bready parts" (the interfaced sides of the T-shirt) will face each other. You can match same-color triangles or mix it up, making one side one color and the other side another color. Pin together each "pizza" slice to keep them matched together throughout Step 6.

6. It's time to design your banner! Use a large work surface (the floor may work better for longer banners) to play around with the pieces, arranging them in a variety of color combinations—show off your creative genius! Just line up the triangles next to one another, flat sides at the top, upper corners touching (like a kid's drawing of upper teeth). Once you decide on your final color palette and layout, it's time to make it permanent.

7. With your banner still laid out on your work surface, lay the cotton rope along the top of your banner, leaving about a foot of rope on each end of the banner, enough to tie it in place when you're all finished.

8. Once your rope is in place, lift up the "pizza crust" and set the rope inside the two pieces of pizza, about 1 inch from the top of the crust. Using straight pins, pin along all 3 sides of the triangle, also pinning the rope in place. Continue to pin the pizza slices along the rope, next to each other with the corners touching, until you have pinned your entire banner to the rope.

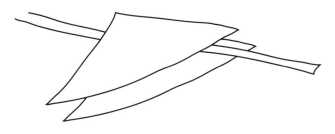

7. Now it's time to sew! Using a large zigzag stitch, sew all 3 sides of the triangle, leaving a 1/8-inch allowance from the edges. Take it slow when you sew across the top, where the rope is located. Better safe than sorry—take your time!

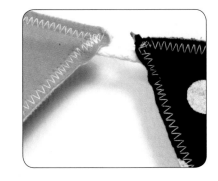

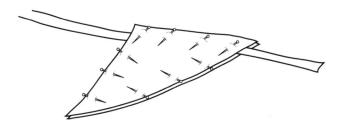

Now you have a fabulous, fun, colorful flag to hang at any festive occasion—or use it as a room decoration for your favorite kiddo!

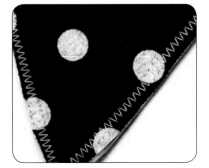

CHILLY GIRL JACKET

Even though I live in Texas, I'm one of those people who always seems to feel cold, so I often find myself reaching for a wrap, despite the hot weather. My passion for wearing tank tops, combined with the local passion for ice-cold air conditioning, means I have to be prepared for any climate.

While trying to come up with the perfect but portable solution, I made several experimental jackets and cardigans out of perfectly cozy cotton jersey. Jersey can be a challenge to sew, but look at it this way: If you use a T-shirt, half of the sewing is already done for you! Plus, if you add some interfacing to an old tee, you'll find it's much easier to stitch up. Whether you decide to create something tailored or keep it casual, this handy warm-up is sure to keep your goose bumps at bay.

Jesse Kelly-Landes's passion for fashion has outlasted myriad fleeting interests: archaeology, dancing, Middle Eastern cooking, communicable diseases, reality TV…you name it.

While teaching herself web development, she used her sewing hobby as the basis for creating online content, not really thinking anything would come of it. Much to her surprise, the orders started rolling in, and now her once-small project has become her profession. She began her own clothing company, Amet and Sasha (ametandsasha. com), in the fall of 2002.

These days, Jesse spends her time dreaming up new clothing ideas, agonizing over the minute details of running a small business, and wondering what's for dinner.

DIRECTIONS

What You'll Need: 2 White T-shirts (one that fits and one about a size larger than you normally wear), 2 packages of black fabric dye, Dark gray thread, One 12-by-12-inch piece of fabric you love, One 6-by-6-inch piece of iron-on interfacing, Loop turner

1. Following the instructions on the dye package, dye the two shirts black. The shirts will come out a rich charcoal gray color, not quite black.

2. On both shirts, measure 12 inches down the back from the neck and mark that point with tailor's chalk.

3. Using a straightedge ruler, draw a horizontal line across both of the shirts at the 12-inch point. Cut straight across the horizontal lines you just made, removing the bottom piece of both shirts.

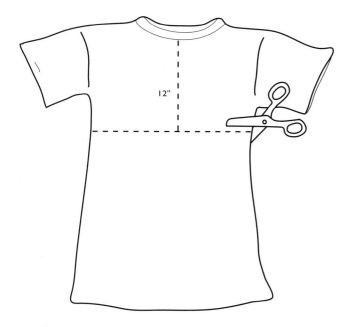

Along the front bottom edge, measure horizontally to determine the center of your T-shirts. Mark with tailor's chalk, then measure 2 inches on either side of that center mark. At these 2 points, draw 2 lines perfectly perpendicular to the bottom edge of the shirts. Cut along both these lines, but only through the front sides of both T-shirts, which will create a cardigan look.

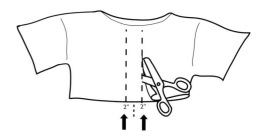

4. Cut the neckband off each shirt, being careful to make the edges as smooth and even as possible. Save the neckbands.

5. Cut the hemmed edges off the sleeves, carefully snipping just next to the hemstitch so that the edges are smooth and even. You can toss out the sleeve edges, or put them on the nearest unsuspecting domestic pet (they'll think you made them something).

6. Turn the larger T-shirt inside out. Tuck the smaller shirt inside this shirt, lining up all seams and edges, right sides facing each other. You'll now be able to cut both shirts at the same time, and they'll match exactly!

8. Leaving the shirts as is, with their right sides facing each other, pin up all the raw edges, except around the sleeves. Stitch all pinned areas at a 1/2-inch seam allowance.

9. Turn inside out, being sure to turn out all corners and edges evenly. Using an iron, press the seams and fabric.

10. Using the shape template on the following page as a pattern, cut 2 pieces out of the interesting fabric you've been saving and 1 piece of the iron-on interfacing.

11. Iron the interfacing to the wrong side of one of your interesting fabric shapes. Pin the 2 shapes right-sides-facing, and sew along all but one edge. Turn inside out and press. Tuck in remaining raw edges and slipstitch closed.

12. Now the neckbands (the ones you were supposed to save, not the ones you put on the dog): Trim them to a 10-inch length, and then turn them both inside out to hide the raw edges. Be patient—this may be a little tricky. I highly recommend using a loop-turner, which can be purchased cheaply at any fabric store.

13. Lay the neckbands, still inside out, horizontally and parallel across the front of the shirt. Pin them evenly on either side so that 1 1/2 inches of each side of the neckbands overlaps the jacket lapels. Stitch in place in a rectangular pattern.

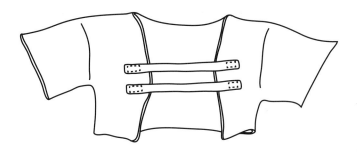

14. Place the shape you made out of interesting fabric beneath the parallel neckbands. Stitch in place.

Now, go find a chilly place and show off your new creation!

SHAPE TEMPLATE

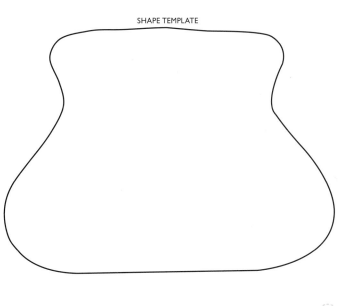

ANGORA GOAT TEE

by Klein Reid

Life is all about contrasts. We wanted this T-shirt to be cheap, and yet luxurious; ridiculous, and yet fancy; macho, and yet feminine; Marlon Brando, and yet Ed Wood. Since we have zero ability in the knitting department, this project seemed like the perfect way for the non-knitter to make something sweater-ish.

Pick out a T-shirt (old and trusted or brand-new, but washed) and choose a great yarn. We went with angora—something super-girly to contrast with the T-shirt. Hot tip: The thicker the yarn, the quicker it will be for you to make the sweater.

James Klein and **David Reid** began collaborating in 1993, hand-making elegant vases, *objets*, lighting, and serve-ware (and more recently soft goods and crystal). Soon after, they founded KleinReid (kleinreid. com), a Brooklyn-based porcelain design studio renowned for the fine, "from scratch" craftsmanship of its pieces. KleinReid's products retail in design stores, museum shops, and stylish boutiques worldwide.

James and David have also created designs for other companies, including Dansk and MGlass, and have been the subject of profiles in many magazines, newspapers, and television shows around the world. In 1999, KleinReid worked with revered designer Eva Zeisel to produce 6 curvaceous flower vases, a dream collaboration come true.

DIRECTIONS

What You'll Need: Embroidery hoop, 2 skeins of angora or other fluffy yarn, Large-eyed needle, Pre-washed T-shirt (we used a men's ribbed tank top)

1. Using an embroidery hoop, frame a section of your tee's front. Double a long length of yarn through your large-eyed needle, and knot the ends together. Following the T-shirt's ribbing, weave the yarn through the hooped fabric in 1-inch running stitches. Work up one rib, and then down the next, covering all the fabric in the hoop. To create a more "woven" look, stagger a simple straight stitch so that the ends of the stitches don't line up horizontally. The stitching can be improvised— tight and controlled, or larger stitches for a looser, fuzzier look. You can also try other stitch patterns, such as herringbone or wave.

2. As you complete a section, move the hoop to an unfinished area, overlapping a bit with what you've just finished. Continue stitching with doubled lengths of yarn, tying off each finished length on the inside of the shirt. We found it best to not stitch right up to the edge of the embroidery hoop, as this can sometimes cause bunching in the fabric.

3. Cover the shirt on the front (and back if you like). When you get to the bottom or side edges of the T-shirt, it's best to tie a knot at the end of each row on the inside of the shirt, before starting up the next row. This will keep the shirt from gathering.

Once you're finished, be sure to follow the care instructions of the yarn that you used, which might mean dry-cleaning your T-shirt. Yes, it's more trouble, but it's so worth it to have a delicious, homemade, angora tee! Yum!

FRILLY DRESS TEE

by ★ Tina Sparkles

DIFFICULTY LEVEL

I wanted to make something super-cute, and yet easy and comfortable to wear in the hot Texas summer. Wearing T-shirts all the time becomes boring, so turning a tee into a frilly dress made perfect sense to me.

I love how this dress is so geometric in style and construction. You don't need a pattern; just start with basic shapes, do some math, and customize it to your body type. I also love that there are so many possibilities for variation using the same principles. You can dramatically change the look of the dress by changing the location (and the amount) of the elastic rows along the tube top. You can change the shape of the skirt by adjusting the amount of gathers and/or the length of the hemline. Fully customizable and cool in the heat...what more could you want from a tee?

Tina Sparkles makes cute, rockin' accessories for hipsters, rock stars, and dorks at heart, specializing in funky guitar straps, belts, and cuffs. She sells them on her website Sparkle Craft (sparklecraft. com), and in stores around the globe.

When Tina gained notoriety for her arty wall hangings, she quit her corporate job to devote herself full time to making sassy crafts. Her flair for fashion can also be seen in her clothing line, presented in an annual fashion show, "Stitch," that she co-produces with some of her fellow Austin Craft Mafia (austincraftmafia.com) members. Tina Sparkles also co-hosts *Stylicious* on the DIY Network. A passionate supporter of women-run businesses, bands, labels, artists, and media, she supports dudes doing great things, too!

DIRECTIONS

What You'll Need: T-shirt in a size that fits you, Sewing machine with serger (or zigzag stitch), 2 yards cotton or lightweight fabric, 8 yards of 3/4-inch lace trim (approximately 1 yard per row), Needle and thread (to match lace), 4 yards of 1/4-inch elastic (approximately 1/2 yard per row)

Preparing the T-shirt

1. Start by making the tube-top bodice of the dress. Smooth the shirt on a large work surface and, using chalk, draw a straight, horizontal line just below the armpits. Cut along the line, through both layers of fabric, to remove the top portion of the shirt. Discard the top (or save it for another project). Trim the length of the shirt so that if you were wearing it as a tube top, the bottom hem of the shirt would hit your waist, where you will attach the skirt.

2. Turn the shirt upside down, so that the hemline of the T-shirt is now the top of the tube top, and serge (or zigzag stitch) along what is now the bottom hem of the tube top, cleaning up the raw edge of your cut line.

3. The next step is to mark off the rows for your decorative lace trim. I made 8 rows of lace, but if you're taller or shorter than I am (5 foot 4 inches), you might want to do more or fewer. The 1st row will run along the top of the tube top, and the last row will be where the tube top connects to the skirt—stick as many rows as you'd like in between these 2 rows. Using tailor's chalk, create guidelines all the way around the tube top for each row.

4. Use the measuring tape to measure across each guideline. We'll call this figure the "Lace Length." Then subtract 1/2 inch from the original number, and we'll call this figure the "Elastic Length." Add 1 inch to each of these numbers, and then write them down somewhere safe, where you won't misplace them (not on your hand, silly— put it somewhere that you won't lose it, like with your keys).

Preparing the skirt

1. Using a measuring tape, measure around your natural waistline, and then multiply the number by 2 1/2; we'll call this measurement "W"—write it down! Next, measure from your waist to the place where you want your skirt to end; we'll call this measurement "L"—write that one down, too. I recommend creating a below-the-knee skirt, but this could work as a mini-dress, too.

2. Now you'll be creating your skirt out of the cotton fabric. Cut a rectangle of fabric to the dimensions of W by L. Serge (or zigzag stitch) along all the raw edges of the fabric.

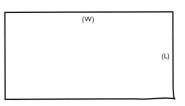

4. Along the top edge of the skirt, sew 2 parallel rows of basting stitches (long stitch length), side-by-side, about 1/4-inch apart and leaving a 1/2-inch seam allowance.

5. To gather the skirt's waistline, gently pull on the ends of each basting thread. Keep gathering until it is 1 inch longer than the bottom row of your tube top, and then stitch along the top of the skirt to secure the gathers.

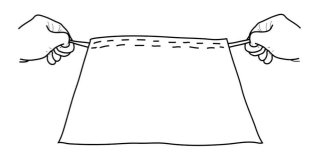

6. Now that you have a rectangle of skirt fabric with a gathered top, it's time to sew it into a skirt. Fold the fabric so that the right sides are facing and the sides meet. Pin the sides together, and then sew them, leaving a 1/2-inch seam allowance. Press the seam open.

Oh, you are so already halfway there, I swear!

Putting it all together

1. Turn the tube top inside out, and then smooth it on your work surface, top-end up. Spread the skirt (still inside out) inside the tube top, and then line up the gathered edge of the skirt with the bottom hem of the tube top, right sides facing. Pin the tube top and skirt together all the way around the waistline. Stitch them together using a serger or zigzag stitch.

2. Now that the top and the bottom of your dress are united, you're ready to gussy up the bodice by adding rows of fluffy, lace trim. Cut 8 pieces of lace to the Lace Lengths determined in Step 4 of "Preparing the T-shirt."

3. Turn the whole dress right side out. Pin strips of lace onto the guidelines you marked on the bodice. Using a needle and thread, topstitch the lace onto the shirt along each row.

4. Cut 8 pieces of elastic to the Elastic Length you determined in Step 4 of "Preparing the T-shirt." You might want to make the elastic shorter or longer, depending on how fitted you want your tube top to be at each row. Test the elastic around your body for comfort. Using tailor's chalk or pins, mark each piece of elastic into 4 equal sections. (Hint: if you're using pins, you'll be using 3, not 4.)

5. Turn the dress wrong-side out. Using tailor's chalk or pins, divide the shirt into 4 equal sections by marking the side seams, center front, and center back.

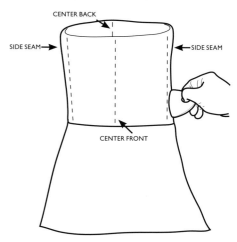

6. Following the stitch lines you created when you topstitched the lace in Step 3, sew the elastic onto the tube top. Stretch the elastic as you sew, so that the marks you made on the elastic match up with the marks you made on the T-shirt.

7. Turn your dress right-side out. If it needs it, touch it up with a dry iron.

Slip on a pair of canvas high-tops and your new dress, and then head to the prom—don't forget your tiara!

KIT-TEE

by ★ Angela Adams

DIFFICULTY LEVEL

M

100% COTTON
SEE REVERSE FOR CARE

This cute kitty was inspired by a special, handmade felt cat that the mother of my associate creative director made for her when she was a baby. I am a huge cat lover and thought this stuffed cat project would fit my Wedding T-Shirt to a T. I made that shirt from a couture rug called "The Wedding Ring" that I designed to symbolize my marriage to furniture designer Sherwood Hamill. The icons depict objects or images that we share or love.

Angela Adams is known for the sense of timelessness, simplicity, and balance in her designs, which are inspired by the remote and harsh natural beauty of life off the coast of her native Maine.

Early in her design career, Angela fell in love with the process of hand-tufting rugs, a technique she reinvented to fit her own aesthetic. Her innovative approach and dynamic patterns helped to establish her quickly as a leader in contemporary design (angelaadams.com).

Recent product additions through partnerships with Architex, Ann Sacks, and Chronicle Books include woven fabrics, upholstered furniture, tiles, and stationery. Angela is constantly exploring new mediums as she expands her collection to create a design-inspired lifestyle.

DIRECTIONS

What You'll Need: Chipboard or stiff paper, Pencil, T-shirt of any color or design, Polyester fiberfill, Embroidery needle, Quilting needle, Embroidery floss (various colors), Decorative details (such as craft jewels, felt or ultrasuede scraps, buttons, rickrack, or any other trim that appeals to your sense of whimsy)

1. On the chipboard or stiff paper, draw the outline of a cat. Use the cat I made as a model, design your own kitty, or download something traceable from the Internet. Your only caveat is that your kitty must fit on the front of your T-shirt. Once you are happy with your drawing, cut it out.

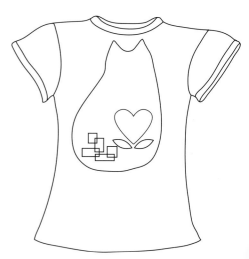

2. Turn your tee inside out, smooth it onto a flat surface, and position your template on the front of it. Use the tailor's chalk to trace around your template.

3. Remove the template and pin the two layers (front and back) of your tee together; use as many pins you need to make sure the layers don't slip around when you cut out your kitty.

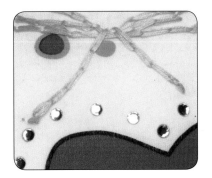

4. Following your template shape, cut through both front and back of your T-shirt, leaving a 1/2-inch margin around your chalked outline.

5. Using a small zigzag stitch, sew 1/2 inch away from the edge of the fabric, following your original chalked line. Leave a 3-inch gap somewhere—the bottom is a good place.

6. Turn your kitty right-side out, iron flat, and then stuff with polyester fiberfill stuffing.

7. Hand-sew the open, 3-inch seam. You now have a very nice kitty pillow, ready for decorating!

8. Using felt, ultrasuede, or other interesting fabric, cut out various decorative shapes. Begin with the eyes, and let your creative energy flow. Hand-sew your embellishments, using a quilting or embroidery needle, as necessary, for ultimate adorability.

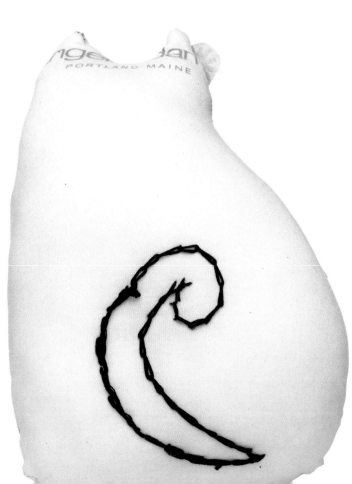

PILLOW FIGHT!

Here's an easy way to turn sentimental faves into cozy yet functional conversation pieces. The coolest thing about turning a treasured tee into a pillow is that you get to rediscover old favorites from the back of your closet and enjoy them every day. Old tees are super-soft and almost always have a story behind them. If you're fickle, try creating a pillow using the front sides of two different tees—that way you can flip them over for a quick change.

For this project, I chose to use a funky, old T-shirt from an electrical contracting company. I thought it would be especially striking to dress it up with girly, pink, pom-pom fringe and a pink flower for added irony. It's enough to make an electrical contractor blush!

I've created two sets of instructions: one for the sewing-savvy among us and another for those who may not be so nimble with the needle. You can jump into this project even if you've never owned a needle and thread in your life.

Leah Kramer might be a mild-mannered computer programmer by day, but in her free time, she's a self-confessed craft junkie who often leaves trails of sparkles and scraps in her wake.

Leah fused her two talents in 2003 to create Craftster (craftster.org), the first online community for subversive crafters and midnight glitterbugs. Craftster has become a vital source of information and inspiration for creative types everywhere, as well as a forum where they can exchange ideas and tips.

Leah also finds time to help organize the wildly popular, not-your-grandma's craft fair, Bazaar Bizarre (bazaarbizarre.org), an annual winter event in Boston. She's also a co-owner of Magpie (magpie-store.com), a Boston boutique that sells hip goods handcrafted by local artists and crafters.

DIRECTIONS

What You'll Need: T-shirt that goes great with your couch, Spray starch, Fringe, Ribbon, Silk flowers or other decoration (optional), Fabric glue, Polyester fiberfill

1. First, lay the T-shirt out flat and iron it well. It's a good idea to use some spray starch to stiffen it up a bit so it will be easier to cut and sew.

2. Next, use tailor's chalk and a ruler to mark off a square that's about 1 inch bigger than you'd like your pillow to be.

3. Place some pins here and there to hold the front and back of the T-shirt together. Cut along the chalked lines, through both layers of fabric, creating 2 squares. The pins will help keep the front and back in place as you cut, so that the 2 squares are the same size when you're done.

4. Pin the 2 squares right-sides together, and sew all the way around the pillow, leaving a 2-inch opening on 1 side. If you're using a sewing machine, choose a long, straight stitch so the fabric doesn't bunch up as you sew.

5. Turn the pillow right-side out by pulling it through the unstitched opening.

6. Use fabric glue to attach fringe on 3 sides of the pillow, leaving plain the side with the opening. I know you're excited, but you have to wait for the fabric glue to dry. Now would be a good time to walk the dog, make some tea, or starch the rest of your wardrobe.

7. Once the glue is dry, you can start inserting polyester fiberfill stuffing into the pillow through the unstitched opening. There's no rule here—make it as full or as flat as you want.

8. Stitch up the opening by hand and glue on the last piece of fringe.

9. If you'd like to add more pizzazz, stitch on a few silk flowers or other decorations.

Shebang! Now put that sucker on the couch and stand back to admire your work.

DIRECTIONS

What You'll Need: T-shirt, Spray starch, Fabric glue, Fringe/ribbon/silk flowers/other decoration (optional), Polyester fiberfill

1. Cut 2 matching squares out of your T-shirt by following Steps 1 to 3 above, but for this version, make sure the squares are about 3 inches bigger than you'd like your pillow to be.

2. Keep the 2 squares wrong-sides together, make sure they're lined up, and pin them together.

3. Instead of sewing the T-shirt fabric together to make a pillow, you're going to fringe it together. To make fringe, cut strips 2 inches long and about 1/2-inch wide all the way around the pillow. A fabric rotary cutter is handy for this step, but sharp scissors will work fine. Use whatever tools and talents the craftin' gods bestowed upon you.

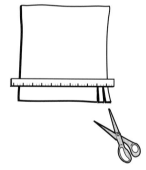

6. When you're done cutting the fringe, cut away a square from each corner. The height and width of the squares should be 2 inches, the same as the length of the fringe (I know this sounds confusing, but I promise it'll all make sense once you get started).

7. Tie each strip of fringe on the front of the pillow to the corresponding fringe on the back of the pillow. Leave some fringe untied at the top so you can insert the polyester fiberfill stuffing.

8. Stuff the pillow to your heart's content, and then tie together the remaining fringe.

See? Who says you need to know how to sew? Rock on!

BOYFRIEND TEE

by ★ Stephanie Kheder

What is it is about guys and their endless obsession with T-shirts (and sneakers)? Spring purging leaves me with tons of extra-large hipster tees to somehow reuse. The Boyfriend Tee is meant to be fun and sexy, customized to your liking. Cut up a great big shirt and make it hot! Attaching accessories adds a funky fashion edge.

It's all about recycling—I made the beaded strands I used in this project by using bits of chain connected with beads and eye pins, embellished with dyed jade and vintage materials. I used the tie from a pair of pajama pants for the back—the color and size were just too perfect.

I dare you to wear your new creation out on a date with your man and see if he recognizes his old shirt!

Stephanie Kheder, designer and owner of Bocage (bocagenewyork.com), opened her Lower East Side notions boutique to bring sophisticated materials to eclectic downtown artisans. The shop emerged in January 2004 as a constant work in progress, and her unique collection of vintage and specialty craft materials grows daily.

Midwest-born Kheder began studying the fine and decorative arts at a young age and never stopped. Today she continues designing accessories, teaching classes, and hoarding new treasures with which to fill Bocage.

DIRECTIONS

What You'll Need: Your boyfriend's T-shirt (or any oversized tee), 1 yard of cord or ribbon, Beaded chains or ribbons for embellishment

1. Lay your tee flat, face down, on a flat work surface. Set your ruler on the tee horizontally, so that each end touches the bottom point of the right and left underarm seams. Trace this line in tailor's chalk. Next, flip the ruler perpendicular to the line you just made, centering it in the middle of the shirt. Use the tailor's chalk again to draw a line from the horizontal line to the bottom hem of the shirt. You should now have a T-shirt with a large "T" written on it.

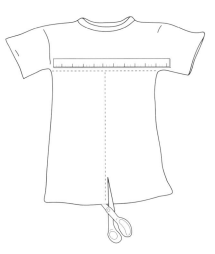

2. Use the scissors to cut the lines you just drew, opening the back into 2 flaps.

3. Flip the shirt over, and lay it flat again. Cut a sexy neckline (ha-cha-cha!) to your desired taste, working off the original neckline as a guide.

CUT FRONT ONLY

4. Begin to create the straps. Using the tee's shoulder seams as a guide, cut the sleeves off, leaving about 1 or 2 inches of fabric on each side of the new neckline. Be sure to taper down at a suitable angle to give your halter its shapely shape.

5. Next, lay the shirt facedown and finish cutting the ends of the straps. You'll be leaving the shirt's shoulder seams intact, extending the "straps" you just made when you removed the sleeves and cutting the back of the tee into 2 ties you'll

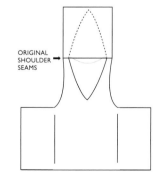

ORIGINAL SHOULDER SEAMS ➡

fasten around your neck when you're wearing the halter. This sounds terribly confusing, but a quick peek at the diagram will illuminate everything. Handy tip: Cutting in a "U" shape or on the bias can give your straps a swirl.

6. Try on the shirt, and pin the "back flaps" together for your desired fit around your midriff.

7. With the tee flat and facedown again, use the tailor's chalk to mark the width you just measured; unpin the shirt. Fold each flap in, using the marked width as your fold line and keeping the bottom seams even.

8. You will now be creating the back casing, 2 fabric "tubes" through which you'll thread ribbon or cord to create a gathered—or "ruched"—back for the halter. Pin the flaps together in place, with the folded-over ends on the inside. Using a sewing machine, make 2 lines of stitching on each flap, about 3/4 inch in from each folded edge. Trim the excess fabric, leaving about a 1/2-inch seam.

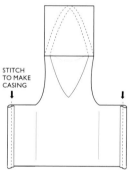

STITCH TO MAKE CASING

9. Using the bottom seams of the tee as a starting point, align the 2 casings together, and use a tight zigzag or buttonhole stitch to connect them, forming the back of the halter. You may need to trim the fabric if the top edges don't line up.

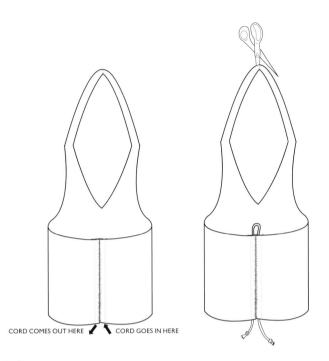

CORD COMES OUT HERE ↑↑ CORD GOES IN HERE

10. Now, create a ruche (or gather) by running ribbon, cord, or long pieces of T-shirt material up through 1 casing, out the top end of the "tube," and then down through the other casing "tube," so that the ends of the ribbon, cord, or pieces of tee fabric dangle from the bottom of the shirt. Gently pull the cords tight, scrunching the back as much as you want, and tying the ends at the bottom to secure in place.

11. Create layered strands of beaded chains or ribbon in whatever length you prefer. Instant jewelry!

12. Finally, stitch the ends of your chains into shoulder seams of the tee, so that the U-shaped strands fall over the front of the shirt. Strands may need adjusting, but should hang naturally and comfortably so you can rock it well.

MARILYN TEE

by ★ Shula Melamed

I came up with the idea for this most glamorous T-shirt incarnation in the least glamorous of ways: I was in my fifth-floor Lower East Side Manhattan apartment doing major housecleaning in the middle of the summer. It must have been at least 90 degrees outside, and it felt like an oven in my un-air-conditioned abode. I needed a suitable cleaning uniform that blended form, function, proper ventilation, and adequate coverage—so as to avoid giving my roommate a heart attack. Out of desperation, I found a shirt a friend had abandoned on a recent visit and started cutting. After a few snips and some creative knotting, I had a totally sexy halter top fashioned out of a piece of material that was formerly fit only to clean windows! Hello, Marilyn in Hanes and terry tennis shorts!

I started playing around with shirts of various sizes. Smaller ones created smaller, bikini-like tops, perfect for wearing to the beach with bottoms or with a gypsy skirt and flip-flops. As a woman who likes variety, I make sure to design things with at least five wearing options.

Shula Melamed's desire to design was borne out of the need and necessity to never, ever wear the same thing as anyone else. After years of perfecting and self-testing her own designs, she is comfortable and excited by the idea of everyone wearing what she has on—especially if she has created it. Her creations can be found at shuladesign.com.

DIRECTIONS

What You'll Need: T-shirt that fits you (for a blousier shirt use a larger shirt; for a bikini top use a smaller shirt)

1. Smooth your T-shirt face-up on a flat work surface. Make a horizontal cut through both layers of fabric, from one underarm side seam, straight (or as straight as you can) to the other underarm side seam. Save the top for another project.

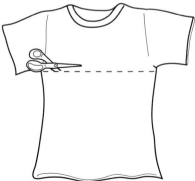

2. Turn the bottom part of the shirt inside out, and cut off the entire side seam on one side. If your shirt doesn't have a side seam, just cut a straight line along the fold of the shirt where the side seam would be. Keep the fabric closed, still folded in half, as it was when you cut it.

3. Cut a parallel line about 2 1/2 inches up from the bottom hem, cutting through both layers of fabric. Stop cutting when you get to the halfway point of your fabric rectangle. Open up the fabric and wonder how the hell you are going to possibly make anything useful or attractive out of this weird-looking thing.

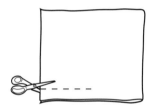

4. Now it's time to knot up your little halter. This procedure is a little difficult to describe, so check out the pictures and diagram. Start by holding the fabric at points A and B, with panel C in front of your chest. Tie A and B together behind your neck, leaving a slightly floppy "cowl" of fabric along your chest. Now tie C and D together behind your back. See?

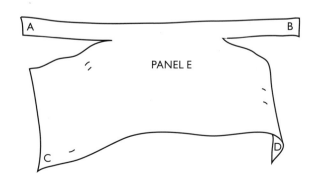

Bikini Option

Instead of knotting the shirt with a cowl front, knot the same piece of fabric into a cute bikini top. Hold in the fabric as if it were a towel you were wrapping around yourself after a shower, with Panel E on your back and A in your left hand and B in your right hand (see photo). Reach up and tie A and B together behind your neck, so that the straps go under your armpits, then up behind your neck. Again, this is hard to describe, but easy to understand when you look at the pictures. Now tie C and D together between your breasts. Either tuck in the floppy ends of your knots or let them hang out. Adjust as needed for Marilyn Monroe bikini-top styling.

Now slip on a pair of terrycloth shorts, and head out into the hot, hot heat.

BLUEBIRD ON MY SHOULDER

by ★ Jenny Hart

Whenever I stitch on a tee, I always embroider a little birdie on my shoulder—tweet and simple. But there's a reason you don't see much embroidery on T-shirts: The fabric is notoriously difficult to stitch on, although it can be done (and these tips will help you). If you find stitching on a T-shirt too frustrating, even with stabilizer, try this alternative: Embroider the pattern onto a separate piece of non-stretchy fabric (even in a different color), and then stitch the piece of embroidered fabric—like a patch—onto the T-shirt. Lovely! I kept this pattern small so you can retain your sanity, and so you have something more to be proud of on your tee than "I'm With Stupid."

Of course, as with most DIY projects, you should feel free to make this one your own. How about embroidering a few lines from your favorite song to float out from the bird's beak? First write the lyrics on a blank sheet of paper, and then trace them with carbon paper—just as you did with the bird pattern—and your bird can sing!

Jenny Hart, best known as the founder of Sublime Stitching (sublimestitching.com), is a pioneer of hip, updated embroidery. Her cheeky designs have helped fuel the DIY revolution and have given veteran needleworkers something new to stitch about. She is also a best-selling author, a widely published embroidery artist, and an illustrator whose stitched and sequined pop-culture portraits have been shown in galleries worldwide.

In addition to authoring and illustrating two publications with Chronicle Books—*Stitch-It Kit* (2004) and *Stitch-It Book* (2006)—Jenny is a judge on *Craft Corner Deathmatch* on E! and the Style Network. Jenny is also a member of the Austin Craft Mafia (austincraftmafia.com), a Texas-based collective of crafty ladies.

DIRECTIONS

What You'll Need: T-shirt, Hardcover book, Photocopier access (to copy the pattern), Dressmaker's carbon paper (available at sewing stores), Ball-point pen, Tear-away iron-on stabilizer fabric, Embroidery hoop, 6-strand embroidery floss in several colors, Embroidery needle

1. Photocopy the bird pattern at 100% size.

2. Eyeball your shirt and decide where you would like your bird to sit. At that spot, slip a hardcover book inside the T-shirt, and set the carbon paper on the top of the shirt, carbon-side down; place the pattern over it. With me so far?

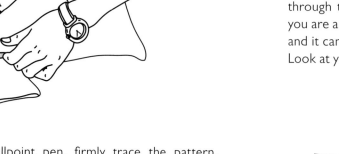

3. Using a ballpoint pen, firmly trace the pattern, transferring the pattern to the shirt via the carbon paper. Be very careful not to shift the pattern while you're tracing it—take your time, and pin that sucker down if you need to!

4. Once you've finished tracing the pattern, turn the T-shirt inside out, and then iron the stabilizer on the back of the fabric so that it covers the area to be stitched. Turn the shirt right-side out again.

5. Center the patterned area of the tee, with the stabilizer underneath it, over the bottom section of the embroidery hoop and place the top section of the hoop atop the fabric, setting it firmly in place and making a smooth, drumhead-like surface on which to stitch. Be careful not to overstretch the fabric.

6. Cut a length of embroidery floss (I used blue, but you can use any color you find appealing), and separate 2 or 3 strands. Thread the needle with those strands.

7. From behind the hoop, bring up your needle through the fabric along the pattern line, and then down again, through the fabric, to the back side. Come up again through the stitch you just made, and continue. If you are a novice stitcher, this is called a "split stitch," and it can be used to embroider the entire pattern. Look at you, you're embroidering!

8. When you've finished stitching the whole pattern, completely remove the stabilizer paper from the fabric by simply peeling it away. Some bits 'n' pieces may stubbornly remain, especially around the stitches, but you'll want those off, too. Be gentle and take your time, and you'll get that paper off *toot sweet*.

9. You're all done! When you launder your tee, don't use hot water or a hot dryer setting, or your shirt might shrink and cause the birdie to bunch up.

If this does happen, don't fret. Simply dampen the fabric or iron it on a steam setting, against the back side from the center out.

Note: *Other types of iron-on stabilizer use water-soluble adhesive, so be sure to read the directions on the package before you purchase it—make sure the stabilizer is tear-away! You will not be able to embroider T-shirt fabric without stabilizer or interfacing of some sort, so do not skip this ingredient! Ask for it at craft and fabric stores.*

T-SHIRT BOXERS

by ★ Logan Billingham

DIFFICULTY LEVEL

XL

100% COTTON
SEE REVERSE FOR CARE

I started turning T-shirts into other things because I would often end up with a T-shirt that was great in some way, but also unwearable. Either the pattern was too zany or unfit for the eyes of the public, or the whole shirt was weirdly shaped or possibly missing a sleeve. This actually happened in high school, when I discovered one of my favorite T-shirts under the kitchen sink after its right sleeve had been used to polish some salad tongs. Tragic.

These boxers are a useful solution to the faulty-T-shirt plague in your closet.

Logan Billingham, a longtime crafter and transformer of clothing, lives in Brooklyn, where she tinkers around with various stuff and plans for the future. Her hobbies include architecture and website programming.

DIRECTIONS

What You'll Need: Photocopier access, T-shirt, 1 yard of 1/2-inch wide loose elastic

1. Using a measuring tape, find the circumference of your waist and write down the measurement.

2. Increase the pattern on a copy machine, so that the reference line is the same measurement as your waist size. Cut out the 4 individual pattern pieces.

3. Take your clean shirt and smooth it onto a large, flat work surface. Cut off the sleeves, right along the seam, where they connect to the shirt. Set the sleeves aside, but don't throw them away. Next, cut along the shirt seams that run along the top of the shoulders, from the sleeve holes to the neck hole. Now your shirt is like a big tube, open at the top and bottom. Slice up 1 side of the shirt and unfold it completely to make a single, rectangular sheet.

T-SHIRT BOXERS PATTERN

WAIST SIZE REFERENCE LINE (example: if you want a 32" waist, enlarge image until this line is 32" long)

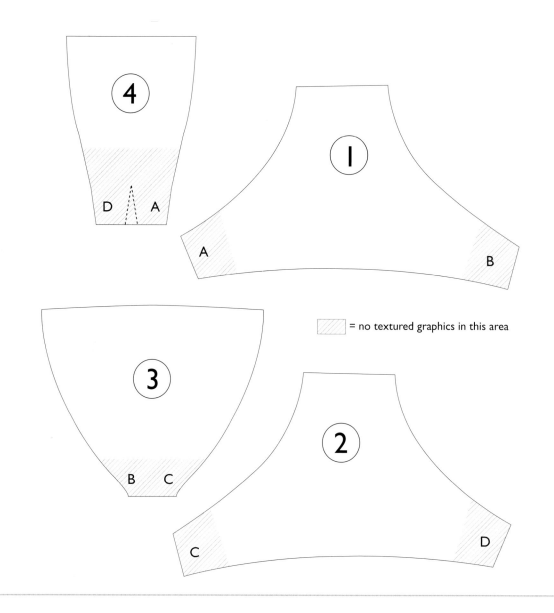

= no textured graphics in this area

4. Smooth your shirt onto your flat work surface, front side up. Now begins the process of determining which pattern pieces will be cut from which parts of the shirt. This will take a few minutes of good, hard thinking (don't hurt yourself) about different options and configurations. Think about where you'd like any graphics to go on your boxers—avoid placing the hatched areas of the pattern over any graphics that might have a thick texture.

5. Once the pattern pieces are in place, pin them down, and then cut around them. Be careful not to stretch or distort the fabric as you cut.

6. Remove the paper patterns from the fabric. Put a pin or some other marker on the "A" side of the leg pieces, so that you can be sure things are properly aligned later.

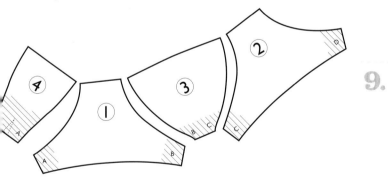

7. Arrange the pieces right-side up (see diagram above). Take the center piece (the front) and fold it in half the long way, right-side inward. Sew a dart at the bottom, taking in about 3/4-inch of fabric total (3/8-inch in from the folded edge). The dart should be less than 2 inches long.

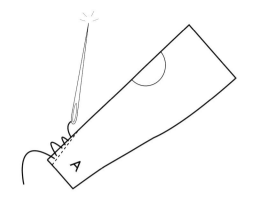

8. Set the center piece aside, and then get ready to pin. Start by taking the left piece and matching it to the right piece, right sides together. The edges won't appear to line up, because they're different shapes, but they're approximately the same length—you're gonna have to trust me on this one. Pin the pieces together at the top, bottom, and middle, and then fill in a few more pins in between. (Go crazy!) Using a sewing machine, stitch the pieces together along the side you just pinned, leaving a 3/8-inch seam allowance.

9. Unfold the 2 joined pieces and spread them on the table. Are the right sides still facing up? Everything look okay? Good, then pin the next piece, and then sew up that seam. After the 3rd seam, it's time to bring the far edge of the last piece around to the first piece. (Your boxers will start to look like boxers at this point!) Be sure to keep the right sides together, and then repeat the pin-and-sew process.

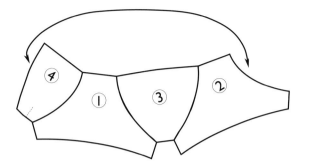

10. Now you have a boxer-shaped tube. Turn it inside out, and smooth it flat on your work surface, with the front facing you. Pin the crotch closed along the bottom edge, starting in the middle and working your way to either side. Turn the garment right-side out and marvel at what should look very similar to a pair of boxer briefs. You are almost there.

11. The final step is adding the waistband, which might seem a little trickier than the piece-of-cake sewing you've done so far. Hang in there—once you get started, you'll see that this part is really easy, too. Find the sleeves that you put aside earlier. Snip along the seam that makes each sleeve a loop, open them up, and lay them flat on your work surface. Your mission is to trim the sleeve pieces into rectangles that are 3 inches wide and as long as possible. When you have 2 rectangles, sew them together on the short ends to form 1 very long rectangular strip, which needs to be long enough to go around the waist of the boxers. Compare the 2

and check. If the waistband strip isn't long enough to match the length of the waist of the boxers, you'll have to take some scrap material and add an additional piece to make the waistband strip long enough. Once your waistband is the correct length, you can sew the 2 short ends of the waistband together to form a closed loop. You might want to take a little rest or snack break to get ready for this next part.

12. Now, pay attention. Turn your waistband right-side out, so that the seams are on the inside. Make sure your boxers are right-side out as well. Insert the waistband loop into the waist of the boxers, until the upper edges are even. Pin the waistband to the shorts all around the top edge, and then stop and check—you should have the right side of the waistband against the inside, wrong side of the boxers. Okay? Okay! Now sew along the edge with a 1/4-inch seam allowance, stretching the fabric as much as you can as you sew. When you're done, flip the waistband up, so that it's outside the shorts. Your boxers should be right-side out, with the waistband attached to the top edge, wrong side out. Fold the top of the waistband down 1/4 inch (towards the outside of the whole garment, as if you are folding down your socks), and pin all around. Whew!

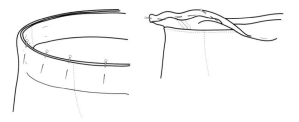

13. Now grab your elastic and wrap it around your waist, making it as tight as you want your boxer waistband, and then stick a pin in the elastic to mark where you'll cut it, and remove the elastic from your waist. Pin the edges of the elastic together, cut off the excess, and sew the ends together using a zigzag stitch. Take this loop of elastic and place it around the boxer waistband, close to the bottom edge, where the waistband attaches to the boxers. Make sure it doesn't twist. Still with me?

14. Ideally, the elastic loop will have a smaller circumference than the waistband, so it will pinch in and make the waistband crumple a bit. Fold the top of the waistband down over the elastic all around the waist. Fold it down enough so that the un-sewn edge (which is already folded over and has pins in it) covers the ugly seam that attaches the waistband to the shorts. Once it's in position, take out the pins, one at a time (but keep that edge folded over), and use each pin to secure the folded edge to the shorts. You are almost done!!!

15. The final step—be careful, this may be tricky: Take your garment, which now looks a heck of a lot like a pair of boxer briefs (except that it's full of pins), and sew the folded edge of the waistband down, all the way around the shorts. Remember to stretch the fabric as much as possible as you

sew, and do not sew the elastic—let it stay free-floating inside the waistband tube.

16. You may want to hem the bottom of each leg if the fabric curls. If not, you're done!

Now get out there and strut your stuff!

I came up with the idea for this shirt when I realized my dream of opening a boutique in New York City. Having wiped out my savings to pursue this dream, I found myself on a nonexistent budget for clothing, yet in a position where I needed to look innovative on a daily basis. Cutting up and reconfiguring T-shirts I already owned was the perfect solution. When customers began to ask where they could buy ones like those I was wearing, I started teaching them to make their own shirts.

Refashioning a T-shirt is a great way to convey your individual style without breaking the bank—plus, you'll never see someone else walking down the street wearing one just like yours.

For this project, all you need is an oversized T-shirt that you'd like to cut down to size. At first, these instructions may look like one long math problem, but don't be put off! Making this shirt may require some simple math, but there's no sewing at all, so go forth and conquer!

Cal Patch is one of the original renegades of the new craft movement, and T-shirt transformation is her specialty. In 2002, Cal co-founded MAKE Workshop (makeworkshop.com), the creative corral for craft-minded New Yorkers. Of all the subjects Cal teaches at MAKE, her T-shirt class is the most popular, largely because no previous skills are required.

Formerly a designer for Urban Outfitters, Cal has also owned a small boutique that sold goods handmade by local NYC artisans. She has her own line of handmade garments, hodge podge, which she sews, crochets, prints, embroiders, and embellishes at her home studio in Brooklyn. She lives with her Chihuahua, Gertie, who has many tiny T-shirts of her own.

DIRECTIONS

What You'll Need: Tape measure, T-shirt

1. First, a little math to make sure the shirt fits right. Using a tape measure, determine your bust circumference at its fullest point. Subtract 1 to 2 inches if you want your shirt nice and clingy, or use the measurement as-is for a less-fitted look (you can always make it tighter later).

2. Now lay the T-shirt flat and measure its width. Double this number to get the full circumference of the shirt. From that sum, subtract your bust measurement, the number you calculated in Step 1.

   Note: *For this project to be successful, you'll need at least a 6-inch difference between the shirt's circumference and your bust size. If your difference number is less than 6, find a bigger shirt.*

3. To find your own personal magic number, divide the number you calculated in Step 2 by 4. Write it down, because you'll need it in Step 10. Okay, no more math—promise!

4. Open the neckline of the tee so the front is to one side and the back to the other. On a table, lay the neck area as flat as you can and use tailor's chalk to draw a "V" neckline on the front half of the T-shirt. Then, cut out the neck.

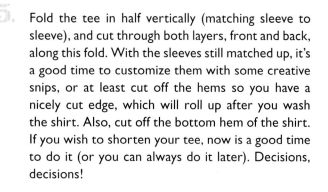

5. Fold the tee in half vertically (matching sleeve to sleeve), and cut through both layers, front and back, along this fold. With the sleeves still matched up, it's a good time to customize them with some creative snips, or at least cut off the hems so you have a nicely cut edge, which will roll up after you wash the shirt. Also, cut off the bottom hem of the shirt. If you wish to shorten your tee, now is a good time to do it (or you can always do it later). Decisions, decisions!

6. Separate the 2 halves of the shirt and fold each piece so that the 2 front edges touch and the 2 back edges touch.

7. Using chalk or pen, mark along both center-front cut edges every 3/4 inch, starting 3/4 inch below the neckline and ending about 6 inches from the bottom. Repeat this step along the center-back edges.

8. Now you'll need that magic number you came up with in Step 3. Draw a line the length of your shirt using your magic number to determine the line's distance from the center-front and center-back cut edges. Cut over to the line at each of your 3/4-inch marks.

9. Tie each 3/4-inch strip to its corresponding mate on the other side. You will be tying fronts to fronts and backs to backs, so don't get confused!

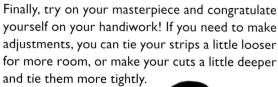

10. Finally, try on your masterpiece and congratulate yourself on your handiwork! If you need to make adjustments, you can tie your strips a little looser for more room, or make your cuts a little deeper and tie them more tightly.

PUNK ROCK CHAIR COVER

by ★ Shannon Roberts

My paternal grandmother ran the family cattle ranch in Montana until the late '50s, when she traded in her saddle to begin a very successful interior design career in Seattle. My earliest memories of Grandma Ruth center on crafting, creating, and building. She once made a tufted footstool from recycled oatmeal containers and tapestry fabric! Ruth, more than anyone, influenced my passions, career, and drive to craft.

Grandma changed the covers on her dining-room chairs the way most women of her time changed the bed sheets! After inheriting her dining room suite, with the chairs covered in white velveteen embroidered with lime-green Chinese characters, I continued the tradition in my own punk-rock style. I have crafted past covers from thrift-store leather coats, discarded fashion-industry yardage in printed blue leopard and silver foil, and now indie band T-shirts. Vive le rock, Grandma R!

Shannon Roberts is a textile designer and knitter based in Brooklyn, New York. Born into an exceptionally crafty family, she began at a young age to knit, sew, and explore the world of do-it-yourself. When she was 8 years old, her grandmother taught Shannon how to re-upholster the dining room chairs she would eventually inherit.

Shannon's knitted artwork has been featured in *Fiber Arts* magazine, in shows around New York, and on knitty.com. For rebellious knitting inspiration, check out Shannon's website, Punk Rock Knitting (punkrockknitting.com).

DIRECTIONS

What You'll Need: Chair with padded seat, Flathead screwdriver, Needle-nose pliers, Masking tape (optional), Logo T-shirt (make sure it will fit well over the seat of your chair), Staple gun

1. Remove the screws that attach the seat to the chair, and then remove the chair seat.

2. With the screwdriver, pry off the staples that are holding the old fabric in place on the padded chair seat. If the staples are stubborn, use needle-nose pliers to rip those puppies out and free the padding.

3. Once you get the staples out, remove the old, yucky fabric cover—but keep it nearby, because you'll need it in Step 5. Try to keep the padding in place so you won't have a big mess later on, when you're reupholstering the chair.

4. Cut the T-shirt up the center of the back to the neckline. Cut the tops of the sleeves open, from the neck down the shoulder. You will now be left with one large, slightly odd-shaped piece of jersey tee fabric. Smooth it onto a large, flat work surface, right-side down.

5. Retrieve the old fabric chair cover, lay it on top of your T-shirt fabric, and pin the 2 pieces together, making sure the tee's logo, graphic, or pattern will fall where you want it to on your chair seat. Use the old fabric cover as a template to cut the new cover from your tee, and then discard the tee scraps and the old cover.

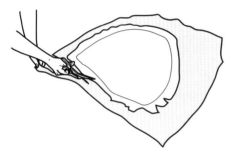

6. Smooth out the tee again, right-side down. Take the padded seat and center it on the tee, padding-side down, wooden seat-back facing up. (If your padding is all messy and falling apart, reverse this step, set the tee on the padding, and flip the whole thing over.) Make sure your tee is still positioned correctly on the seat cover.

7. Now you're going to staple down the fabric. Begin with the top edge of the tee, stapling the fabric firmly into the wooden seat back. Start with one staple in the middle of the fabric edge, and then a few more on each side, working back and forth to staple the fabric evenly to the seat back. Gently pull the bottom edge up, and then staple it in place. Repeat with the right and left sides, making sure you are pulling the fabric evenly on all 4 sides. Staple the corners, moving the fabric into folds.

8. Trim off the excess fabric. Reattach the seat to the chair, using the original screws.

Now sit down in your new favorite chair, and have yourself a little rest. You've earned it!

NOT-YET-DEAD-KENNEDY GARDENING APRON

When it comes to crafting, I'm all about recycling. Making your own stuff should be way cooler and at least marginally cheaper than anything store-bought. Plus, reusing clothes destined for Goodwill leaves you with a chunk of change to put toward a guilty pleasure.

I've had this Kennedy boys T-shirt hibernating in my closet since the mid-'90s, when big was better. By today's standards, it's too oversized and haggard to wear, but—AHA!—when reworked into an apron, I have Bobby, Jack, and Ted on hand whenever my tomato plants need a trim.

Traditional gardening aprons aren't even delightfully tacky— they're just plain ugly. It's good to know that with minimal sewing skills, you can make a ruff-'n'-tuff apron fit for a gal as stylin' as Jackie O—just by using that much-loved big tee and a pair of worn-out pants. Ethel would be so proud.

Gayla Trail is a designer, author, and artist, as well as the creator of the acclaimed gardening website yougrowgirl. com. After five years online, Gayla wrote and designed a handy and clever gardening book, *You Grow Girl: The Groundbreaking Guide to Gardening*, published by Fireside/ Simon & Schuster (2005). Her writing and photography have also been featured in magazines and books throughout North America.

Gayla lives in Toronto, where she and her partner, Davin Risk, run their design studio, Fluffco (fluffco.com). In addition to client work, the team designs products and handmade goods sold through their online store SUPERfantastico (superfantastico.com).

DIRECTIONS

What You'll Need: Large T-shirt, Rotary cutting tool, Fusible webbing, 1 pair of cords or jeans, Pinking shears (optional), Lace or fancy edging (optional)

1. With a pair of scissors or rotary cutting tool, cut the hem from the bottom of the T-shirt.

2. Smooth the T-shirt out onto a flat surface. Measure 2 1/4 inches from the bottom and cut a straight line across the shirt. Set this piece aside for now—you'll use it later as an apron tie.

3. Cut the remaining T-shirt in half at the side seams, leaving you with a separated front and back.

4. Smooth the front half of your tee out onto your work surface once more. Cut the remaining piece into a rectangle that measures 20 inches by 15 inches. Set aside the leftover scraps.

5. Starting at the top left corner of your rectangle of fabric, measure 11 inches down the edge of the left side and mark the spot with tailor's chalk or pencil. Cut a diagonal line across beginning at this dot and ending at the bottom corner on the right side.

6. Ladies and gentlemen, start your irons! Iron the front half of your T-shirt to a piece of fusible webbing of the same size.

7. Now that you've created a lining for your apron, you need to cut a matching outer piece. Using scissors, remove a leg from a pair of old cords, cutting just under the rear-end part where the leg portion begins. The goal is to use the widest part of the leg (remember, pants with a flared leg may be wider at the ankle instead of the thigh).

8. Slice this tube open, following along the inside seam. Flatten the fabric on your worktable with the outside of the fabric facing up.

9. Align your lining piece (the T-shirt portion) face down with the piece of pants fabric, so that the right sides face one another, and secure them together with pins. Cut the pants fabric down to match the lining piece in size exactly.

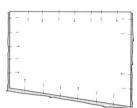

10. Sew a 1/4-inch seam around the edges of the triangle, leaving a 5-inch opening along the right-hand side for turning the piece right-side out. Use pinking shears or scissors to cut excess fabric from each corner.

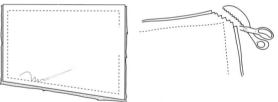

11. Turn the piece right-side out and iron it flat. You are so close to being finished.

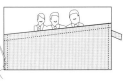

12. Following the slope, sew a 1/4-inch seam straight across the diagonal side. This will be the top seam of your pockets later on.

13. Lay the piece flat, lining side up, with the diagonal side on the bottom, and fold the bottom up, leaving a 3-inch space of lining fabric peeking out at the top. More lining fabric should show on the left side since the bottom edge was cut on a diagonal.

14. Pin up the left and right sides. Sew a 1/4-inch seam along each side from the top all the way down to the fold. Now you have a rectangle with a large, slanted pocket. You're almost there!

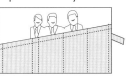

15. To finish, divide the big pocket into smaller pockets of varying sizes. Make as many pockets as you want, reserving the taller, right side for long-handled tools and the shorter side for small stuff, like markers and seed packets. Starting from the left side, measure and then mark straight lines onto the fabric with tailor's chalk. Begin each line at the top of the pocket and mark down to the bottom fold. Following the chalk lines, stitch your pockets in. Now you're officially done with the apron body.

Making the Tie

Welcome to the home stretch! The only thing left to do is stitch on a tie along the top edge of your apron to hold it to your waist. Here's a golden opportunity to get creative, because you can make a tie from just about anything: a long piece of twill tape, ribbon, or sturdy decorative trim. If you'd rather be thrifty and resourceful, you can make your own tie using the T-shirt loop you set aside back in Step 2. Simply cut through the loop to make a long piece of T-shirt material.

The tie should measure at least 1 1/2 to 2 yards in length. To make a longer tie, cut another piece from the longest edge of the leftover T-shirt fabric and sew the pieces together. Back up over your stitches a few times to make them good and strong. If the T-shirt you're using is old and thin, you'll need to reinforce it with a piece of fusible webbing before moving on to the next step.

Fold the bottom up 1/2" and press

FOLD LINE

Repeat with the top edge.

FOLD LINE

Fold in half and press again.

FOLD LINE

1. Lay the T-shirt strip on the ironing board, and then fold the bottom up a 1/2 inch and press flat. Repeat with the top edge. Now fold the top down to match up with the bottom and press again.

2. Open the tie up and fold it over the top edge of the apron body, positioning the body at the approximate center of the tie. You don't need to measure; just eyeball it. Affix the tie with pins, and sew it onto the apron body, following a straight line about a 1/2 inch from the edge.

Now get that apron on and run out to the garden to show it to your plants. They'll be so impressed!

FRINGED CARNIVAL CLOWN

by ★ Sarah Neuburger

DIFFICULTY LEVEL

S

100% COTTON
SEE REVERSE FOR CARE

These fellas are fashioned after the old carnival clowns you find at state fairs. Although I was never any good at the midway games, the graphic designs and posters have always caught my attention—as did the disgustingly greasy carnival food.

While these clowns are one-of-a-kind art pieces, they can also be useful in practical ways. Try them as doorstops, decorative bookends, or even pin cushions (though that does seem kind of mean). However, what they probably do best is just stare into space, making you wonder what they're thinking about.

Heavily silk-screened shirts work best for these critters, since the ink stops the shirt from fraying. It's also a great way to keep your favorite tee around even after holes have long since made the armpits fully ventilated hemispheres. Now you can tell people that old T-shirts are some of your best friends.

Sarah Neuburger has more "treasures" than any one person should probably own, because she loves to spend hours searching through racks of clothes at thrift stores. After spending several years in New York City, earning her MFA from the School of Visual Arts, she's back in the South, hitting flea markets and garage sales early on Saturday mornings. During the rest of the week, she makes large-scale drawings, artist's books, mixed-media photographs, and other household goodies.

The Small Object (thesmallobject.com), a cottage industry for Sarah's limited-edition oddities, features delightful doodles with an eccentric, quirky reexamination of everyday items. She believes that good things do come in small packages, and the most significant moments can be the most mundane.

DIRECTIONS

What You'll Need: T-shirt, Cardboard (two 10-by-5-inch pieces), Measuring tape, X-Acto blade (optional), Buttons and other embellishments, Fabric glue, Polyester fiberfill (optional)

1. To create your clown template, draw a 9-by-4 3/4-inch bullet shape onto cardboard. Using scissors or an X-Acto blade, cut out your template. Set the template onto your T-shirt, and using tailor's chalk, trace around the shape. Be sure to choose the section of your T-shirt that has the best design for the front of the clown. Using sharp scissors, trim around the template, cutting through both layers of tee fabric.

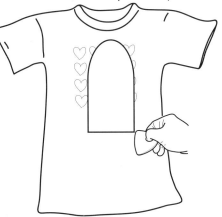

2. Now that you have the body of the clown, it's time to figure out the face. Get creative, and use pieces of leftover T-shirt, buttons, additional fabric, and so forth. I stitched on a blue, oval face using a blanket stitch (if you don't know what this is, Google it or pick up a beginner's embroidery book), but you could simply topstitch (ditto) or glue on your clown's face. I added 2 circular eye rounds using vintage fabric scraps, and then 2 matching buttons for the eyes, a wood-grain button for the mouth, and 2 stacked buttons for the nose. He's a crazy vintage clown!

3. Now that your clown has a face, you can sew up the body. Topstitch around the shape, 3/4 inch from the edge, leaving the bottom open so you can stuff it later.

4. Cut the fringe around the clown in the 3/4-inch perimeter, being careful not to cut through your stitched seam. Try to cut super-thin fringe, as close together as possible, each fringe strand about 1/4-inch wide.

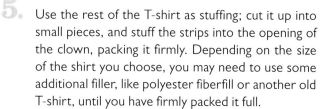

5. Use the rest of the T-shirt as stuffing; cut it up into small pieces, and stuff the strips into the opening of the clown, packing it firmly. Depending on the size of the shirt you choose, you may need to use some additional filler, like polyester fiberfill or another old T-shirt, until you have firmly packed it full.

6. To close up the bottom of the clown and make it stand up, you'll need to make a cardboard base. Measure the diameter of the hole in the bottom of the clown, find a glass or object with the same diameter, and trace it onto to a piece of cardboard. Trim the cardboard around the circle and discard the scraps.

7. Insert the cardboard round into the bottom of your stuffed clown, and then stretch the bottom of the shirt to cover it. Pin the fabric in place, stitch it closed, and trim off any extra fabric on the base so that the clown will stand upright. You're done!

Now all you have to do is think of an appropriate clown name...

BEADED
LADY

Years ago, at a thrift store, I found a bead loom with a half-worked project still on it, so I bought it and figured out the technique just by staring at the work-in-progress. I designed this T-shirt project with that thrift-store bead process in mind.

Whitney Lee started latch hooking when she was nine years old, but didn't start hooking the sexy stuff until she was in her early 20s. She started her web-based business, Made With Sweet Love (madewithsweetlove.com), as a way to make her work accessible to a large audience.

Whitney has had major solo art shows in Toronto, Chicago, and her hometown of Columbus, Ohio. Her artwork has been published in magazines around the globe. She has appeared on *SexTV*, a television show that respectfully explores sexuality and gender in an intelligent way, as well as on several episodes of *Uncommon Threads*, a how-to show about hip needlecraft projects.

Whitney lives in Austin, Texas, with her husband, PJ, and their son, Peyton.

DIRECTIONS

What You'll Need: Pre-washed T-shirt, Fabric-marking pencil, Rotary cutter, 2 craft organizers, Label stickers, Upholstery thread to match your shirt, One pack each of 6-by-9-millimeter-barrel Craft Etc. brand pony beads in the following colors: Hot Pink Pearl, Red, Cranberry, Ruby Frost, White, Light Pink Pearl, Chocolate, Black, Gray, Silver Sparkle, Tortoise, Hyacinth Frost, Lilac, Dark Purple Pearl, Navy, Black Pearl, Rust, Red Pearl, Two packs each: Ivory Pearl, Ivory, Dark Ivory, Gold Sparkle, Orange Pearl

* * *

1. First, get organized! Label each compartment of your craft organizer with the bead color and pattern number. Now your beads will be organized, accessible, and portable.

2. Turn the T-shirt into a loom. Use the fabric-marking pencil to draw a 7-inch-wide by 10-inch-tall rectangle on your shirt, placed about 3 inches down from the neckline.

3. Using the fabric-marking pencil, divide the top edge into 20 1/3-inch-wide pieces, keeping your marks on the inside of the rectangle. Mark the bottom edge of the shirt in the same way.

4. Using the rotary cutter, cut the right, bottom, and left edges of the rectangle. Be careful not to cut through the back of the tee. Leave the top edge connected to the shirt. Using the ruler as a straightedge, connect the 1st mark on the top row with the 1st mark on the last row, and cut along the ruler edge to make a vertical strip of fabric about 1/3-inch wide. Continue until you cut your rectangle into 20 vertical strips of fabric still attached to the T-shirt at the top.

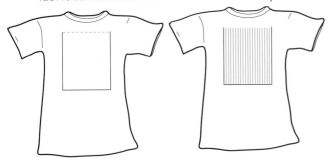

5. Wrap a small piece of masking tape around the bottom of each strip, which will help you get the fabric through the center of the bead.

6. Time to start beading! On the pattern, each square represents 1 bead. The pattern is 20 squares wide, 1 bead for each fabric strip that you just cut. Use the key on the pattern to figure out which bead color corresponds to each number. If you organized the beads in containers as suggested, it'll be a piece of cake. Look at only the top row of the pattern, and put your first bead on each fabric strip accordingly. Push the bead through, all the way to the top of the strip.

16	27	14	31	27	14	31	32	26	16	25	16	25	16	16	16	16	16	16	16
16	31	27	14	31	32	26	18	26	32	16	15	16	15	16	16	16	16	16	16

Key:
- 10 Hot Pink Pearl
- 11 Red
- 12 Cranberry (Crafts Etc.)
- 13 Cranberry (Beadery)
- 14 Ruby Frost
- 15 White
- 16 Ivory Pearl
- 17 Ivory
- 18 Dark Ivory
- 19 Light Pink Pearl
- 21 Chocolate
- 23 Black
- 24 Gray
- 25 Silver Sparkle
- 26 Gold Sparkle
- 27 Tortoise
- 31 Hyacinth Frost
- 32 Orange Pearl
- 38 Lilac
- 39 Dark Purple Pearl
- 40 Navy
- 41 Black Pearl
- 43 Rust
- 44 Red Pearl

7. Before you add any more beads, connect this row horizontally. Start by threading the needle and knotting the end. Come through the back of the fabric on the top left side of the 1st bead. Then, take the needle down through the 1st bead, up through the 2nd, down through the 3rd, up through the 4th,

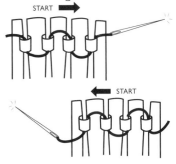

and continue that way until your needle ends up on the top side of the last bead. Send your needle down through the fabric on the top right of the

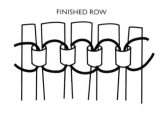

FINISHED ROW

bead, and up again through the fabric on the bottom right. Now weave your needle through the row of beads again, this time in the opposite direction. Go up through the 20th bead, down through the 19th, up through the 18th, etc, until you go down through the 1st bead all the way on the left side. Take your needle down through the T-shirt fabric near the bottom left of that bead, and knot the back. You've completed your 1st row!

Note: On either side of the beaded area is the T-shirt fabric to which you are securing each row. When you send your needle through this fabric, fold it 1/8 inch and go through 2 layers of fabric, which keeps the raw, cut edge hidden and also gives strength to the beaded area.

8. Add the next row of beads, push them up to the top next to the first row, and repeat the process. Beading is time-consuming (but therapeutic), so be patient!

9. Congratulations, you've made it through all 40 rows! Now it's time to finish the bottom of the "loom." Remove the masking tape from the fabric strips. Lay the T-shirt on a flat surface, and arrange the beads so they look good. Using straight pins, secure the bottom of the rectangle to the ends of the beaded strips. To make things easy on yourself, put the pins in vertically, taking the end through the 2 shirt layers and then through the center of the bead, where the thread will eventually go.

10. To thread the final piece together, start at the top left of the 1st bead in the last row, coming through the back of the fabric. Send your needle down through the 1st bead, through the fabric, and then up through the 1st bead again. Go down through the 2nd bead, through the fabric, and up through the 2nd bead again. Continue this through all 20 beads, and finish when you reach the T-shirt fabric on the right side.

11. Hey, you're almost finished! Try on your shirt to see whether there are any holes around the edge of the design. If needed, use your needle and thread to repair each separately, using a couple of small stitches, if necessary. Since the bottom of the shirt is attached only to the last row, your design may tend to separate there. If so, just thread your needle and weave it through the last 6 to 8 rows, using the same technique that you use when beading a single row, reinforcing the vertical connection.

You're finished! Way to go! Now, wasn't your patience worth it? Gorgeous!

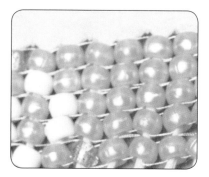

GIDDY
GIDDY TEE

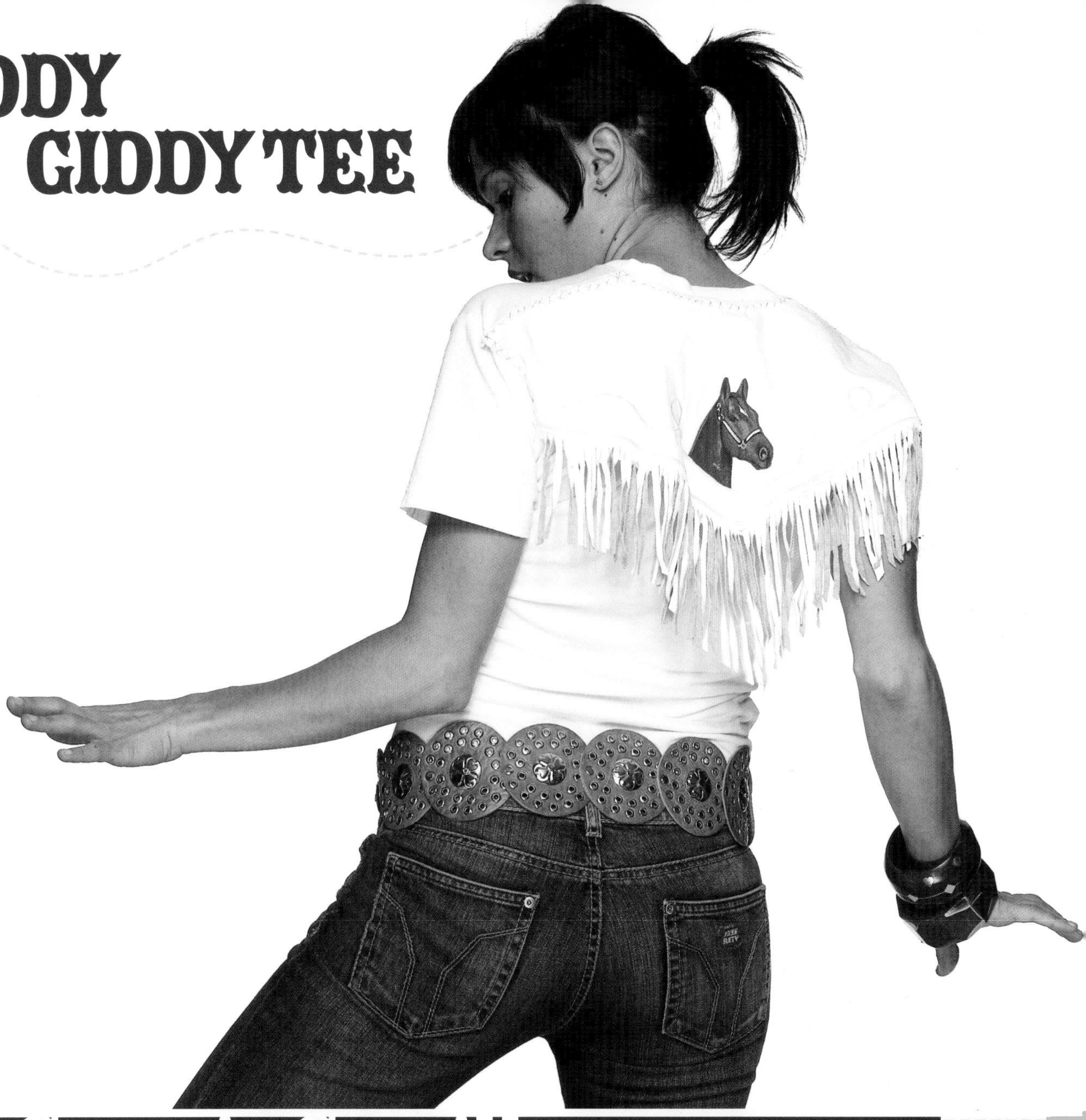

by ★ Georgie Greville

DIFFICULTY LEVEL

While on a road trip out West, I found a rad old Western shirt in an alley dumpster in Aspen, Colorado. It turns out that people in Aspen have pretty nice trash, because there wasn't one stain on the white shirt, white leather fringe, or the hand-painted horse details on the front and back. I tried to work the shirt into my wardrobe when I got back home to New York, but it was just a little too jazzy for the big city. I decided it had to be dressed down a bit, so I cut off my favorite parts and sewed them onto a old, nicely worn, white T-shirt. Now my shirt has the perfect balance of Western and bohemian.

Georgie Greville and her partner in crime, Cressi Parks, make up Two Pop, a music and art collaboration. They live in downtown New York City and like to make things all the time. They create T-shirts in Georgie's Chinatown apartment when they're taking breaks from shooting pictures and films.

DIRECTIONS

What You'll Need: Western shirt with lots of detailing, T-shirt that fits

1. Find a rad Western shirt with leather fringe and back detail—the more detailed, the better, but you can always paint your own detail if you get a plain shirt. Good places to look are flea markets, thrift stores, and vintage shops.

2. Carefully cut off the fringe, back yoke, and any other details that you like from your Western shirt.

3. Trim the fringe to fit the neckline of your T-shirt, and pin it to the tee along the neckline. Trim the Western yoke to fit the shoulders of your T-shirt, and pin it into place. Take any other details that you cut from your Western shirt and pin them into place on the T-shirt.

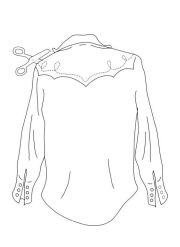

4. Using a cross-stitch, sew the Western shirt details in place.

BACK OF SH:RT

Giddy-up and go to town!

NEAPOLITAN RUG

by ★ Diana Rupp

Some tees are not fashion-makeover friendly, but don't give them the old heave-ho just yet—that's some valuable and well-loved material! Instead, cut them into strips, do a quick connect, then crochet away into the form of a colorful rag rug. Handmade flooring fit for a queen... or a little dog who thinks she's a queen!

You'll need to know the very basics of crocheting to accomplish this project. You can easily find simple, helpful instructions in a beginner's crochet book or online. Don't be shy—try it out! Crochet is really simple, and your results will be stunning.

Diana Rupp was taken under the wings of two great crafters at a young age: her mom, Kathy, and her great-grandmother, Hallie (a professional milliner and expert quilter). Taught to knit, sew, and embroider by the age of 8, she can't remember a time when she wasn't obsessed with crafts.

In 2002, Diana decided to trade the glam and glory of being a starving writer to pursue her real passion: making stuff. She launched MAKE Workshop (makeworkshop.com), a craft school in New York City. As creative director, she spends her days teaching people to make all kinds of things and lining up guest instructors who specialize in everything from shoemaking to silkscreening. It's a dream come true.

DIRECTIONS

What You'll Need: 6 XXL men's T-shirts with side seams removed (I used 2 each in ecru, fuchsia, and chocolate brown), Rotary cutter, Size Q jumbo plastic crochet hook, Tapestry needle (a blunt, big-eyed needle you can find at any craft store that carries yarn)

1. Start by preparing strips of T-shirts and joining them together to make "yarn." To do this, cut the hems off all 6 shirts. Then, using a rotary blade and ruler—or scissors if you're really patient—cut the T-shirts vertically (from bottom to top) into 1-inch strips. Trim each strip before you hit the sleeves or neckline.

2. Next, join the strips by snipping a 1/2-inch slit in one end of Strip 1. Pull Strip 2 through the slit, and then cut a 2nd slit on the far end of Strip 2. Thread the other end of Strip 1 through the slit in Strip 2. Pull it through until it makes a knot. These directions might sound really complicated, but once you try it with actual strips of tee, you'll see it's cake. Continue in the same way until all the fabric is connected, staggering the color for desired effect. When you've knotted all your strips, wind it up like a big ball of yarn—not bigger than your couch, but pretty big.

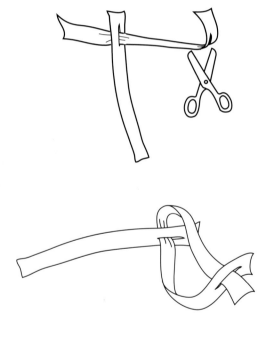

3. To crochet the rug, begin with 4 very loose chain stitches (now is when you bust out the beginner's crochet book). Be sure the stitches are loose—it's super-hard to work with stitches that are too tight.

4. From these first 4 stitches, you will now form the very center of your rug. Use a slipstitch to join the end of the fabric to the bit of fabric just past your 4th chain stitch. Again, this sounds complicated, but it's a cinch. Place a safety pin in at this point as a marker.

5. Continue crocheting, working 8 single crochets into the center of the ring (study your crochet book to see how to attach new crochet stitches to stitches you've already formed). These 8 stitches should form a complete circle around your first 4 stitches. Congratulate yourself…you've just made the center of your rug!

6. Now you're going to start increasing stitches in every round so that the circle will keep getting bigger and bigger. Increasing in crochet is super-simple—you just work 2 stitches in 1 space every time you want to add an extra stitch. If this is still confusing, take another peek at your beginner's crochet book. Here's how your rug will grow:

Row 1: Work 2 single crochet stitches into each chain space (you've already completed this round).

Row 2: Work 1 single crochet into the last chain space, and then, to increase and start a new circle, work 2 single crochet stitches into the 1st chain space of the 3rd circle. Repeat to complete the entire round.

Row 3: Work 1 single crochet into the last 2 chain spaces, and then, to increase and start a new circle, work 2 single crochet stitches into the next chain space to increase. Repeat to complete the entire round.

Row 4: Work 1 single crochet into the last 3 chain spaces, and then, to increase and start a new circle, work 2 single crochet stitches into the next chain space to increase. Repeat to complete the entire round. Getting the idea?

Continue in this same method, doing one additional single crochet before the increase each time you go around the circle. As the rug gets bigger, you will be increasing less frequently because it will take you more stitches to get around the circle.

7. When you've crocheted a rug that is 24 inches in diameter, it's time to finish up. Cut the yarn and secure the end to the crocheted rug with a slip-stitch. Using a tapestry needle or your fingers, tuck in any funky ends and you're done!

One tip: If it seems like the rug isn't flat enough, throw in some more increases—evenly around—until it starts to flatten out again. If it seems like the rug is all wonky and floppy, do a few decreases by skipping spaces. Crocheting is pretty free-form. Feel free to wing it!

EYE BURRITO

by ★ Amy Sedaris

DIFFICULTY LEVEL

S

100% COTTON
SEE REVERSE FOR CARE

One evening, my friend Billy Erb and I decided to make an eye burrito (a small, seed-filled sack that you can refrigerate and then place on haggard eyes to rejuvenate them). Billy asked me for a black T-shirt he could use to craft the burrito. I offered a *Sex and the City* T-shirt. So with scissors, a bit of ingenuity, and plenty of weed, Billy fashioned the T-shirt into an eye burrito.

Amy Sedaris lives in New York with her imaginary boyfriend, Ricky, and her rabbit, Dusty. Her hospitality book is titled *I Like You* (Warner Books, 2006).

DIRECTIONS

What You'll Need: T-shirt (or even a large scrap of tee), 3 contrasting colors of felt, Flax seeds (about 2 cups), Lavender or other soothing dried herbs (optional), Essential oils (optional)

1. Smooth your tee onto a flat work surface. Cut two 5-by-11-inch rectangles out of your T-shirt, which will give you enough material for a nice burrito, as well as a 1/2-inch seam allowance.

2. Using the patterns provided (or feel free to improvise!), cut two "eyes" out of the felt, using one color for the eye, another for the iris, and another for the pupil. Using big stitches (or the sewing machine), sew the eyes onto the right side of one of the rectangles.

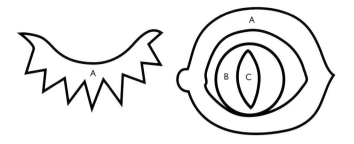

Next, pin the 2 rectangles face-to-face and machine-stitch 1/2 inch from the edge around all sides, leaving a 2-inch opening on one side. Clip the corners off diagonally, being careful not to cut any of the stitching.

Turn the pillow right-side out, making sure the corners turn out nicely, and fill the bag about halfway with flax seeds. When you lay it flat, it should drape comfortably over your eyes. Rice, lentils, or dried peas would also work. You could also add some lavender, soothing dried herbs, or essential oils to the mix.

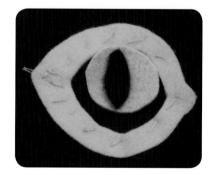

Close up the hole with a few hand stitches.

That's it! After working so hard, you deserve a nice long nap. Drape your new eye burrito over your face and snooze away.

FRESH YOGA – MAT BAG

Let's face it—yoga mats get stinky. Sweaty feet plus synthetic foam equals gross. Most mat bags don't do much to fight the funk, but here's one that does...plus, you can make it out of materials you already have on hand.

Old cotton tees are ideal for making a yoga tote because their absorbent breatheability helps your mat dry out between downward dogs, so it smells less like feet and more like a lotus flower. A few basic crochet stitches are all you need to get you "om"-ward bound; if crochet seems new and scary to you, take a deep breath, pick up a beginner's crochet book, and check it out. Crochet is actually quite simple, even if you've never before touched yarn.

Lenny Williams hails from Texas, a place where revamping stuff to extend its shelf life has developed into an aesthetic all its own. She comes from a long line of crafty types—think coffee-can hanging baskets, crocheted Lone Star beer-can hats, and old suits and dresses made into quilts. Lenny draws inspiration from her resourceful forbears in everyday life, whether she's helping plan an event for work, traveling around the world, or throwing a cocktail party for friends.

After moving to New York City to study acting, Lenny worked as the art director for a public relations firm to pay the bills. She's a freelance PR consultant, which gives her the freedom to volunteer locally and globally, as well as the time to obsess over the baby clothes she crochets for Siamese twins.

DIRECTIONS

What You'll Need: 7 large 100%-cotton T-shirts without side seams, Size F crochet needle, 3 feet of 1 1/2-inch belt webbing, Four 1 1/2-inch D rings, Thread that matches your belt webbing

1. The first thing you'll do is create the yarn you'll use to crochet the bag. Cut the hem off all 7 shirts and put them away to use in a different project. Next, starting from the bottom of each shirt, cut a continuous 1-inch-wide strip—apply the same technique you'd use to peel an apple in 1 long strip. Work your way up the shirt, cutting the strip, and stopping when you reach the tee's armpits.

2. Once you've cut all 7 T-shirts into long strips, pull each strip to make the edges roll up, creating "yarn." Work in foot-long sections, pulling the string taut. Once it's all been stretched, roll each strip into a ball, and you're all set to crochet. How cool is that?

3. Using your size F needle, start a 6-stitch crochet chain. To create a circle out of these 6 stitches, connect the ends using a slipstitch. Continue crocheting around the circle. At the beginning of each new round, add one more chain stitch to accommodate the circle's growth.

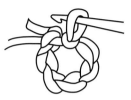

5. Once you have a 7-inch circle, subtract 1 stitch and continue with a single crochet, which causes the row to flip up, starting the sides of your tote bag.

6. Keep crocheting in a continuous, circular pattern until your bag is tall enough to hold your mat, about 22 inches high. Be sure to check the height as you go, since the tee-yarn has a lot of give and stretch (which is the whole point of yoga, right?). When you finish 1 ball of yarn, just tie on the end of the next ball of yarn with a knot and keep going.

7. Once your bag is tall enough for your mat, you'll crochet a ruffled border into the top of the bag. Continue crocheting as before, but work one double crochet into stitch 1, double crochet 5 stitches into stitch 2, and double crochet 1 stitch into stitch 3. Continue all the way around—1 double crochet, 5 double crochet, 1, 5—until you've made a complete row of ruffles around the opening of your bag. Tie off.

8. To make the drawstring tie, cut 3 strips of leftover yarn into 18-inch pieces. Braid these pieces together, and then to secure the braid, tie knots 3 inches up from each end, leaving the ends to tassel. Weave the braid in and out of the row of stitches just below the ruffle.

9. To make the tassel at the bottom of the bag, cut leftover T-shirt material into ten 6-inch pieces of yarn. Hold all the pieces together in a bundle, and tie the bundle tightly together in the middle with 1 of the 6-inch pieces. Loop the end of the tie through the center of the bottom of the bag and tie it firmly to attach all the tassels. (If you're having trouble finding your center, yoga should help.)

Making the Shoulder Strap

1. To make the shoulder strap, spread the piece of belt webbing onto your work surface. Thread 2 of the D rings onto the webbing and then slide them down until they are 7 inches from the end. Fold the webbing over to create a loop, with the D rings inside. Sew the loop closed 1/4-inch below the D rings, leaving a tail that is approximately 6 inches long. Repeat this process to attach the remaining 2 D rings on the other end of the webbing.

2. To attach your strap to the bag, thread the tail of 1 end of the webbing through 1 of the crochet-stitch holes 3 stitches up from the bottom of the bag. Pass the tail back out through the hole above it, and then thread the tail through both D rings, making a loop around the crocheted material. The D rings should be facing out. Next, cinch the webbing as you would a belt by passing the tail back through one of the D rings. Repeat the steps to attach the other end of the shoulder strap to the top of the bag.

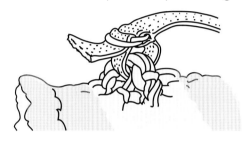

Now run off to class so you can show off your new yoga-mat bag! Très chic!

ROCKET TEE

by ★ Saltlick

Like most of our designs, the rocket came to us randomly. We tend to gravitate toward images that evoke a sense of play or childlike imagination, so we were playing around with icons and images from the 1950s: the TV and the airplane. The rocket ship was a natural evolution; we love that it suggests movement and adventure, and it's a great design for us because it's not just for kids or grown-ups—everyone seems to respond to a rocket ship. With a wink and a nod to the '50s, this design is whimsical and fun—just like the folks who wear our tees.

Jeni Matson and **Yuko Koseki** met in 2002, while working as editors in the film industry. Seeking an escape from the demands of their computer monitors and keyboards, they rediscovered their common childhood affection for sewing and appliqué, traditional women's work taught to them by their respective moms. Soon their collaborative designs generated a buzz among friends, family, and coworkers, and **Saltlick** (saltlicknyc.com) was born. Now, Saltlick boasts a collection of more than 50 designs for men, women, children—even dogs!

Though some of Saltlick's more enterprising patrons have suggested a switch to factory production, Jeni and Yuko continue to hand-sew all their tees personally, using vintage and unique fabrics.

DIRECTIONS

What You'll Need: Prewashed T-shirt, Photocopier access, Fabric marker, Felt (we used gray, navy blue, red, yellow), Fabric scraps (we used orange), Fabric scissors, Lightweight fusible interfacing, Embroidery floss (we used yellow, orange, white), Thread to match fabric and felt

1. Make the pattern by blowing up the design on a copy machine.

2. Using a fabric marker, trace the rocket body onto gray felt, the flame pieces onto yellow and red, and the stripe for the rocket body on the navy blue.

3. Cut out the felt pieces using sharp fabric scissors.

4. Iron fusible interfacing onto the fabric pieces you're using for the rocket ship details. Make sure the coated side is up against the wrong side of your fabric.

5. Trace the pattern for the top panels onto yellow felt and the window onto the fabric backed with interfacing. Cut out the shapes.

6. Using a blanket stitch, embroider the felt window pieces onto the rocket body towards the top to make little panels (see photos for placement). This will secure the fabric to the rocket and also help protect the edges from unraveling. For stitching, use only 3 of the 6 strands of the embroidery floss.

7. To make the window, embroider the orange fabric to the navy blue rectangle with a simple stitch. Using a sewing machine or a needle and thread, attach the window to the rocket body using a standard straight stitch.

8. Position your rocket patch in the center of the tee and a few inches from the neck, and set the navy felt stripe in place. Pin the patch to the T-shirt and stitch all around the edge, about 1/16 of an inch from the edge, fastening the stripe down at the same time.

9. Next, use the sewing machine to stitch details of the rocket in the gray felt.

10. Pin both the red and yellow layers of the rocket-blast together onto the tee and stitch them with a straight stitch using yellow thread.

11. Using the embroidery floss, hand-stitch the final rocket details: sew little dashes in the blue stripe and Xs onto the rocket body.

Ready for blast-off!

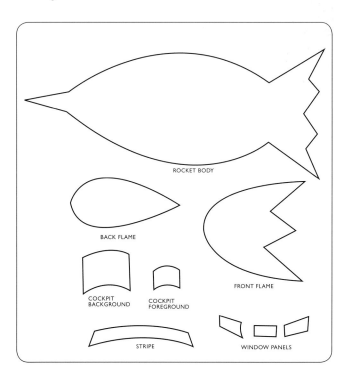

ROCKET BODY

BACK FLAME

FRONT FLAME

COCKPIT BACKGROUND

COCKPIT FOREGROUND

STRIPE

WINDOW PANELS

EASY TOTE

by ★ Amy Sperber

You, too, can have a tote in a flash! Making this bag is as easy as cutting off the sleeves and stitching the bottom of an old tee. Any T-shirt will do—if you need a bigger bag, just use a bigger shirt, silly! Has your Chihuahua been getting lost in your oversized bag? Then use a small shirt to make her ride cozier. (Be sure to make the handle-holes big enough that she can check out the view now and then and let out a yip.)

Heck, if you can turn an old T-shirt into a Chihuahua carrier, then what can't you do? Think, think, think—and put your best ideas to work with this easy-peasy, one-two-threesy tee-tote!

Amy Sperber likes to make things. Back in high school, she made a big old black cape that she wore until she went to college, where she learned how to make things for money. She also made a battle-bot (a robot that fights other robots). Amy makes up one-third of 31 Corn Lane, which is a rad design, craft, and style company. Check them out at 31cornlane.com. Bonus: If you come to Amy's house, she'll make you a snack.

DIRECTIONS

What You'll Need: T-shirt of any size, Beads (optional)

1. Cut the sleeves off your tee.

2. Cut a deep "U" shape at both the front and the back neck.

3. Turn T-shirt inside out and fold it so that the armholes are parallel—almost like it's already a tote.

4. Line up the bottom front and back hemlines of the T-shirt, smoothing out the fabric with your hand. Using a sewing machine or a needle and thread, join the bottom seams of the shirt by sewing a straight line across them. Turn the shirt right-side out again and look it over. You'll see that your shirt has now become a tote bag, with the shoulders of the T-shirt acting as the tote handles. But wait! You're not quite finished…

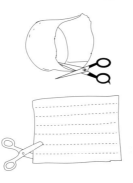

5. Take one of the sleeves you removed in Step 1 and cut it open, creating a long strip of T-shirt material. Cut two long strips from this material, each approximately 1 1/2 inches wide.

6. Wrap these strips around the handles of the tote as reinforcement. Be sure to leave a long end so that after wrapping the strips approximately 8 times around the handles, depending on the length of your strips, you can still tie together the ends to finish.

7. For a more gussied-up look, string some beads onto the ends of the ties and secure them by tying knots in the fabric.

Presto, tote-oh!

ROCKER TEE

It's hard to resist your favorite band's promo shirt, but must they always come in size XL? No need to look like the House of Cotton—with just a few snips and tucks, you can reshape any oversized crewneck into a breezy summer skirt. Here are some tips to make the process flow.

First trick: Shift the skirt you're making onto the bias (a 45-degree diagonal to the direction of the knit), which allows for smart and stylish stretch and drape. T-shirts are normally cut along the grain of the fabric, so turning yours 45 degrees before cutting will automatically set you right.

Trick two: To avoid stitch breaks, pull the fabric ever so slightly as you sew.

The patterns provided are meant as rough guides—you'll want to try on the piece at intervals to make sure it hugs your curves. Vroom!

Todd Oldham is a New York–based designer and photographer. This project originally appeared in *ReadyMade* magazine.

DIRECTIONS

What You'll Need: Measuring tape, Extra-large rocker T-shirt (prewashed), 35-inch piece of 1/2-inch wide elastic

1. Measure your hips in 2 places: 2 inches below your waist (or wherever you want the skirt to sit) and at their widest point. Add 1 inch to each measurement for seam allowance, and then divide each in half to get waist (W) and hip (H) measurements.

2. Fold your shirt on the bias, as shown in the diagram. At the top of the tee, just below the neck, draw a line starting at and perpendicular to the fold. The length of the line should be the same length as the W measurement.

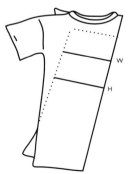

3. A few inches below this line (approximately as far as your widest hip-point from your waistline), draw a 2nd parallel line the length of the H measurement.

4. Add 1 1/2 inches to H, and draw a line of this length as low on the shirt as possible (while still being able to fit it on the wider half of the shirt). This will be the hemline. When you open up the shirt, you should have a triangle-shaped area missing from the narrower side of your shirt. Don't worry—you didn't cut anything wrong. You're right on track.

5. Place the skirt pieces face-to-face, and pin them together. Using a 1/4-inch seam allowance, sew up the long side seam. Use a stretch straight stitch if your machine has it; otherwise, to build some stretch into the seam, pull slightly on the fabric as you sew.

6. To close the triangular gap in the skirt, cut a triangle from the leftover sleeve or shoulder of the shirt. The technical term for this triangle is a "gusset" (just in case there's a pop quiz later).

7. With the skirt inside out, lay the triangular gusset over the triangular gap and pin it down. Then, sew together using a standard straight stitch.

8. Cut a piece of the elastic to the length you originally measured for your waist plus 1 inch.

9. Loop the elastic into a circle and overlap the ends by 1 inch. Stitch the overlapped ends together.

10. Pin the elastic band to the right side, around the waist of the skirt, centering the raw edge of the skirt along the inside of the elastic. Using a wide zigzag, stitch the elastic band to the skirt. The zigzag will keep your stitches from breaking when you stretch the skirt over your hips.

11. Trim the hemline to your desired length.

Voilá! A rockin' new addition to your wardrobe!

VINTAGE BIB TEE

by ★ Heather Sperber

DIFFICULTY LEVEL

S

100% COTTON
SEE REVERSE FOR CARE

I'm always looking at things upside down, and I love to find vintage sewing patterns and illustrations, so when I saw an old pattern for a woven, bibbed shirt, I thought it would be fun to make as a tee. As usual, I didn't know if it would work until I tried it, but I finally figured out a cool way to take that old-fashioned, bibbed-shirt idea and turn it into a happenin' T-shirt. Leave it to your crafty imagination, and something always works out, right?

The first one I made was from a great African-print tee with a wild vibe, but then I decided to go girlier, and this is what I came up with. Since you can use any material and embellishments for this project, you can personalize your tee any way you like. Think sequins, lace, charms—go nuts!

Heather Sperber, a fashion designer in New York City for ten years, designs women's clothing for retailers such as American Eagle and Urban Outfitters. She loves pony paint-by-numbers, cooking, and the crafty community created around 31 Corn Lane.

Online, the Sperber sisters reside at 31 Corn Lane (31cornlane.com). Originally from Exit 109 off the Garden State Parkway, these three spazzy girls—Heather, Amy, and Teeter Sperber—now live in Williamsburg, Brooklyn, where they breed small dogs and craft ideas. Heather and her sisters started making things as soon as they could hold safety scissors, and they haven't stopped since.

DIRECTIONS

What You'll Need: Cotton-jersey T-shirt that fits snugly, One 20-by-20-inch piece of good-lookin' fabric, 1 to 2 yards of rickrack trim, 1 to 2 Yards of 1-inch lace

1. Turn your T-shirt inside out. If it's wrinkled, iron it flat so it is easier to handle. Smooth it onto a flat work surface, front side up.

2. To create the bib, place the square of fabric on top of the T-shirt so that the top of the fabric overlaps the neckline and shoulder seams; flip the shirt over. Using tailor's chalk, trace the whole curve of the neckline, from shoulder seam to shoulder seam.

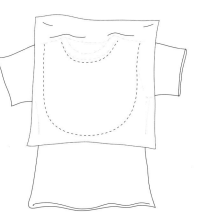

3. Take the fabric off the T-shirt and cut out the traced neckline. To make sure the neckline you just cut is the correct shape, fold the fabric in half, checking that both sides line up. Trim as needed to even out your half-circle.

4. While the fabric is still folded, cut out the shape you want for the bottom of the bib, the part that will lie flat against the middle part of your T-shirt. I chose a round shape, but anything will work for this project—a plunging V-neck, a square, or an off-kilter shape—whatever works for you and your imagination.

5. Open the fabric, and iron it flat. Place the tee, still inside out, front side up, back on your work surface and smooth it flat. Set the ironed fabric on the front of the T-shirt, lining up the neckline-shaped edge to the neckline of the T-shirt, and pin it to the top layer of the tee with straight pins. Smooth out any wrinkles, and pin the rest of the fabric to the T-shirt. Be careful to only pin the bib to the top layer of the tee.

6. Carefully sew the neckline of the fabric to the neckline of the T-shirt underneath. Make sure the tee is still inside out so the seam allowance of the neckline will hide the raw edges of the woven fabric.

7. Smooth out the remaining fabric, and make sure pins are still in place. Sew the remaining fabric to the T-shirt, and you're done!

8. To hide the rough edges of the fabric on the front of the shirt, sew some rickrack onto the bottom and side edges of the bib, following the stitch lines you made when you sewed the bib to the T-shirt. I added rickrack and lace for extra girliness, but you could add buttons or other decorations to reflect your own individual style.

Congratulations! You're vintage stylin', baby!

CUTE CAFÉ CURTAINS

CRAFT.
ROCK.
LIVE.

by ★ Vickie Howell

DIFFICULTY LEVEL

L

100% COTTON
SEE REVERSE FOR CARE

Accidentally shrink one of your favorite tees in the wash? Don't call it curtains just yet! Instead, why not make a curtain out of it? This punk-rock version of the traditional café cutie is a quick and inexpensive way to add some funk to your windows without breaking the bank. Knit up your own ruffle embellishment or sew on some store-bought trimmings—either way, your curtains will make the perfect conversation piece at your next coffee klatch!

Vickie Howell is the mother of two boys, host of television's *Knitty Gritty*, co-host of the DIY Network's *Stylelicious*, author of *New Knits on the Block* (Sterling, 2005) and *Not Another Teen Knitting Book* (Sterling, 2006), and a member of the Austin Craft Mafia (austincraftmafia. com), a Texas-based collective of crafty ladies. More of her designs can be found in publications nationwide and on her website, vickiehowell.com.

DIRECTIONS

What You'll Need: Logo T-shirt, Plain T-shirt, I yard vintage (or vintage-inspired) fabric, Measuring tape, Rotary cutter, I ball off-white worsted-weight yarn, Scraps of red worsted-weight yarn, U.S. size 9 knitting needles, Tapestry needle

1. Cut the sides and neckline off both tees, creating four panels, each about 8 inches by 17 inches. You'll only need 3 of the panels for this project, so you can ditch the extra 1.

2. Cut the vintage-inspired fabric into the following sized pieces: one 36-by-8-inch piece for the top border, two 2-by-22-inch pieces for the curtain stripes, and one 23-by-25-inch piece for the curtain backing.

With right sides facing and alternating shirt and fabric pieces, pin and sew T-shirt panels (placing logo tee in the center spot) to the curtain-strip pieces, and press the seams flat.

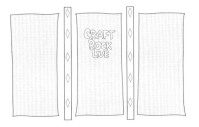

With right sides facing, pin and sew the top border piece to the curtain body you've just created, and press the seams flat. This step completes the curtain front.

With right sides facing, pin the curtain front you've just completed to your curtain backing (the 23-by-25-inch piece of fabric). Sew around all 4 sides, leaving an opening at the top for turning. Trim the corners, turn right-side out, and press.

Fold both layers of the top edge under 3 inches and pin (be sure to fold the raw edges of the turning hole inwards as you go). Using a 1/8-inch allowance, sew the seam. This step creates the curtain-rod pocket.

To Make the Ruffle:

Using the cream-colored yarn, cast on 88 sts.

Rows 1–3: Knit all stitches.

Row 4: Purl all stitches.

Row 5: *Knit 3 stitches, increase 1 stitch (by knitting in the front and back of next stitch). Repeat from * to end.

Row 6: Purl all stitches.

Row 7: *Knit 4 stitches, increase 1 stitch (by knitting in the front and back of next stitch). Repeat from * to end.

Row 8: Purl all stitches.

Row 9: *Knit 5 stitches, increase 1 stitch (by knitting in the front and back of next stitch). Repeat from * to end.

Row 10: Purl all stitches. Cut cream yarn.

Row 11 (wrong side): Join in red yarn and purl all stitches.

Row 12: Knit all stitches.

Bind off.

Pin ruffle to bottom of curtain, and sew on by hand or with sewing machine.

Hang your curtains, grab a cappuccino, and admire your handiwork.

EMPIRE WAIST TEE

by ★ Callie Janoff

This project was born out of one of many "I have nothing to wear" moments. I wanted something flattering but not revealing, feminine but not girly, unpretentious without being blah, and—above all—something I could accomplish in ten minutes with stuff I already had lying around the house.

My motto is "Keep it simple." You can make this project really quickly without any sewing skills or expensive tools. Anyone can handle this project!

Callie Janoff, the co-founder of the Church of Craft (churchofcraft.org) and minister to the New York City chapter, has been making stuff for as long as she can remember. Her earliest toys were raw craft materials, she learned to crochet in Brownies, and her grandma taught her to sew in junior high. Callie went on to make all of her friends' prom dresses, and then earn a BA in Art from UCSC and an MFA from the School of the Art Institute of Chicago.

Callie not only likes to knit, crochet, sew, and cook, she also remodels just about anything she can get her mitts on. She especially likes to make things out of wood, old junk, and paper, but mostly she works on making the Church of Craft cool and fun. She also performs wedding ceremonies and works on her building in Brooklyn.

DIRECTIONS

What You'll Need: Classic men's T-shirt (1 size too large)

1. Trim the stitched hems from the bottom and the sleeves of the tee. Cut these loops of fabric open to make three strips.

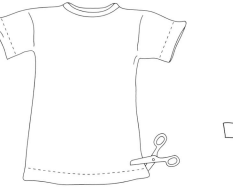

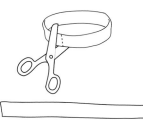

161

Put on the tee. At your lower bra line, just below your bust, where an empire waistline would fall, make two small, vertical marks, about 1/2-inch tall, using pencil or tailor's chalk.

Take off the tee. An inch away from the marks you just made, draw matching marks toward the sides of the shirt.

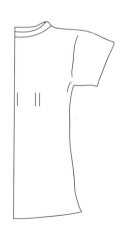

Determine the horizontal center of the tee, and then fold the shirt in half vertically around this center, with your chalked or penciled marks facing out, so you can see them. Next, make two marks a 1/2 inch from the center on either side, in line with the other marks you've made.

Lay the tee flat. Make 2 marks a 1/2-inch on either side of the side seams (or where they would be if you have a seamless shirt), in line with other marks.

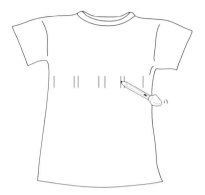

You should now have 12 marks on your T-shirt, running along your bust line. Using scissors, snip all the marks to make 1/2-inch long vertical slits.

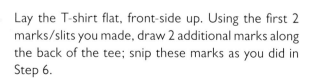

Lay the T-shirt flat, front-side up. Using the first 2 marks/slits you made, draw 2 additional marks along the back of the tee; snip these marks as you did in Step 6.

8. Put T-shirt back on. Make 2 marks where the shoulder seams would be if the shirt fit you properly.

9. Take off the shirt again. Following the shoulder seam down the sleeve, make one more set of marks, about 2 inches from the edge. Snip these marks, too.

10. Now it's time to turn your hole-y T-shirt into an Empire-Waist Tee. Take the longest of the 3 strips you made in Step 1, the hem you cut from the bottom of the tee. Thread the strip through the two slits you cut on the back of the T-shirt, placing the unsnipped seam (if there is one) on the inside of the shirt and pulling the ends of the strip out through each slit.

Weave the strip in and out of the other snips you made, all the way around the shirt. When you are done, the ends of the strip will be dangling out the back slits.

11. Take the other 2 strips from Step 1 and weave them through the arm slits, so that the ends come out the top of the shoulders. Cinch the ends of the strips to gather the sleeve fabric, and then tie the ends of the strips into a pretty bow.

12. Put on your shirt. Cinch the ends of waistline strip, gathering the fabric so that the shirt is snug, but not too tight. Adjust the ties as you please. If your shirt is too long, feel free to trim it to your desired length.

The directions might sound a little complicated, but once you get started, you'll find that they're incredibly easy. When you're finished, your hard work will pay off with a cute, one-of-a-kind shirt that fits you perfectly.

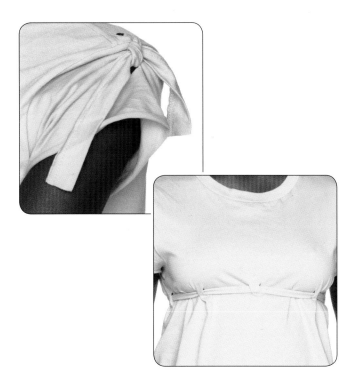

INSTA-SCARF

Simply stylie and cozy to boot, this scarf makes any outfit autumn-riffic in a jiffy. Starting at the bottom hem of your T-shirt, cut 1 long, 3-inch wide strip of fabric, using the same technique you would use to peel an apple into one long strip. Keep cutting the strip until you reach the tee's armpits. Trim to a comfortable length, wind it jauntily around your neck, and go apple-picking.

INSTA-HEADBAND & WRISTBAND

Insta-headband
Complete your outfit with this handy hair accessory. Just cut the sleeve of T-shirt off at the seam. Give it a little stretch and fit it over your head as a headband.

Insta-wristband
Use another cut-off sleeve for an instant, sporty outfit-enhancer. Place the the sleeve around your wrist, lightly stretch and twist the fabric into a figure 8, the loop the fabric around your wrist again. Hot, hot heat!

by ★ Amy Sperber

DIFFICULTY LEVEL

S

100% COTTON
SEE REVERSE FOR CARE

KEYHOLE TEE

On your way out to a show?
Make your tee rock with a few snips. First cut out a boatneck shape at both sides of the top of your T-shirt. Next cut a keyhole shape out of each sleeve and tie the loose ends into a bow knot.

JULIET TEE

Make any boyish tee into a feminine fancy. Simply cut out a princess neck-shape along the front neckline, then cut off the bottom of each sleeve and a couple of slits to make the Juliet sleeves.

TEASE
Acknowledgments & Credits

BIG, HUGE THANKS TO FOUR PEOPLE WHOSE ART AND TALENT MADE THIS BOOK:

Danielle St. Laurent for her extraordinarily gorgeous photography,
Arin LoPrete for enthusiastically rocking the book design,
Julie Jackson for writing her heart out to make *Tease* entertaining, and
Shoshana Berger for crafting the essay that brings it all together.

ENORMOUS THANKS TO:

Michelle Howry, the supportive visionary editor at Perigee, along with the rest of the Perigee posse—
John Duff, Christel Winkler, Jessica Reed, and Craig Burke.

Special thanks to: Jeni Matson for handmaking the Teasiest tee for the book cover;
Amy Schiappa of Fringe for her gifted hair and makeup work; Jenni Lee for her creative styling;
Jessica Garcia for her organizational genius; Cal Patch, the resident craft expert, for always being available
at a moment's notice; Debbie Stoller, Heather Sperber, and Amy Sperber for getting in the boat the first day;
Tamar Love Grande for her ambitious yet patient technical editing; Stephen Conti, for taking on the role
of design ringer and retouching guru; and to Colleen Kane and Emily Gordon for being our last-minute proofing pros.

Extra thanks to: Christine, Bill, and Jen at Picture Ray Studio; John Smith; Mili Simon; Tracy Toler;
Vinnie D'Angelo; and Urban Outfitters for providing all the additional clothing and props for the photographs.

BIGGEST, SLOPPIEST THANKS TO ALL THE CONTRIBUTORS FOR GIVING THEIR BRILLIANCE, CREATIVITY, AND INSPIRATION TO THIS PROJECT.

PHOTO CREDITS:

All photographs except for contributor photos by: Danielle St. Laurent
All additional clothing and props generously contributed by: Urban Outfitters
Styling by: Jenni Lee
Hair and makeup by: Amy Schiappa and Mili Simon
Photo of Jenny Hart on page 105 by: Kenneth B. Gall
Photo of Amy Sedaris on page 139 by: Billy Erb

Todd Oldham's project on page 151 originally appeared in ReadyMade, Issue 11, May/June 2004

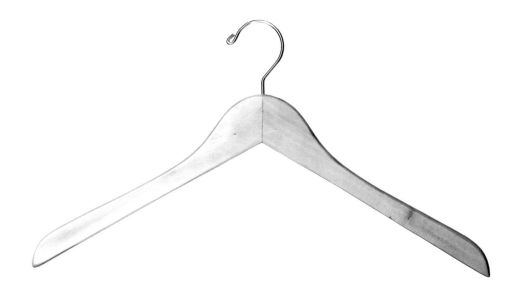